❋
Will You Marry Me?

Will You Marry Me?

Oonagh Armstrong

Thorsons
An Imprint of HarperCollinsPublishers

Thorsons
An Imprint of HarperCollins*Publishers*
77-85 Fulham Palace Road
Hammersmith, London W6 8JB

First published by Thorsons 1994
1   3   5   7   9   10   8   6   4   2

A catalogue record for this book
is available from the British Library

ISBN 0 7225 2930 9

Typeset by Harper Phototypesetters Limited,
Northampton, England
Printed in Great Britain by
HarperCollinsManufacturing Glasgow

To Richard.

Contents

Introduction   ix

Chapter 1   Love and Expectations   1
Chapter 2   Weddings   19
Chapter 3   Role Playing   29
Chapter 4   Money and Careers   45
Chapter 5   Sex   59
Chapter 6   Children   81
Chapter 7   Emotional and Physical Health   93
Chapter 8   Family and Friends   107
Chapter 9   Guidelines for Communication   119

Conclusion   137
Further Reading   144

Introduction

'Will you marry me?' is a question most young girls dream to be asked and indeed, eventually will be. We expect our wedding day to be the 'happiest day of our lives' and we look forward to years of wedded bliss with the person of our dreams.

Despite the social acceptability of co-habitation and single parenthood, marriage remains as popular as ever. Unfortunately, it does not always turn out to be the true path to happiness that we expect and although some people wait until they have lived together for a while, or until they are well past their youth and established in their careers, it does not necessarily mean that their marriage is going to work. Divorce rates continue to rise and more and more families are suffering from the effects of marital discord.

This is a simple beginners' guide to marriage, intended for those about to or planning to get married, irrespective of age or status. It aims to give people about to commit themselves in marriage points to consider before taking that step. The vast majority of first marriages take place when the couple are in their mid-twenties and it is mainly this group that I aim to address, although there is something of relevance for everyone inside these pages, even those wise people who have taken their time and think that nothing can possibly go wrong. Every chapter is relevant; there are occasions when advice will overlap from one section to another and this is because different aspects of our relationships also overlap.

Most people expect their relationships to work and the pain and disappointment that result from divorce can be avoided if consideration is given to various factors *prior* to the commitment itself.

What I have looked at in every chapter are the main reasons why marriages break down. I attempt to guide couples into considering these factors right at the beginning, when the pattern of the relationship is formed.

We make full preparation for many decisions we take - going on holiday, buying a house, applying for a job - and there are ways in which we can seek help and guidance with these preparations. Unfortunately there is precious little guidance given to those about to make one of the most important decisions of their lives: with whom and when to marry.

Seeking counselling and guidance after marital breakdown is becoming more and more acceptable and there are waiting lists for those seeking help with marital problems. Unfortunately, for several couples it is already too late to salvage a broken marriage. How much better, therefore, to make adequate preparation before the decision to marry is reached!

In these days of ever-changing social attitudes and the altering of the role played by women in society, many people are confused as to how to conduct themselves within their relationships. Our whole social set up is geared around the family unit, but the nuclear family of Mum, Dad and two children is slowly but very surely changing and now one in five children will see their parents divorce before they are sixteen.

Women especially need to look very seriously at their place in this world and their roles as wives within that framework. In this book I give advice to the couple collectively but some sections are for the female and male separately. This is because the vast majority of divorce petitions are sought by women and it is they who appear to mould the way in which the relationship develops.

However, as individual as we are, every rule and theory pertaining to a successful marriage can be challenged by the interpretation of those involved. Every relationship and therefore every couple are unique. Decision to act upon advice is up to the individual, but the more information we can gather, the better a position we are in to make decisions. If you are about to marry, please read every chapter carefully and at least consider some of the points raised. Do not be frightened to address these issues; avoiding them now will only serve to create problems later.

Long and happy marriages *are* possible. It has less to do with pure luck than you might think. Love can last forever, if nurtured properly.

These are the ten crucial points to consider:

- Be in love before you marry.

  You should not assume that sexual attraction or mutual interests will be enough. Neither should you 'settle' for someone because you feel you are getting older, your friends are getting married or you think being married will make your life more comfortable. Do not seek to love, rather build on your own self-esteem, career and friendships. Love will always materialize when you least plan for it and expect it.

- Be as honest with your partner as is humanly possible, especially in the first year you are together.

  This is the toughest one of all. In our initial days as lovers we try our best to impress the other person and feel compelled to 'hide' what we consider to be our worst points. But inevitably these will come out anyway, so it's better to let your partner get to know you in your most natural state, without pretence.

- Love and appreciate yourself.

It is really impossible to love anyone else until you love yourself. Loving yourself has nothing whatsoever to do with false pride or arrogance. It is about caring for yourself and being proud of your achievements and plans. We are all of us equal inside and everyone has beauty within them. Seek to love yourself and others will quickly follow suit.

- Be kind to each other.

In years to come it is your kindness to each other which will matter more than anything. We all have to be aware of our own value but it should not lead to total selfishness and a desire to take all from someone and give them nothing in return. At different times in our lives we all experience illness, sadness and loneliness. A kind partner will help us through these times and so a good marriage is built.

- Learn to recognize and trust your own instincts.

If you strongly suspect that something is amiss in your relationship, before you marry, then ignore it at your peril. If you think that a particular aspect of you or your partner's behaviour now may lead to problems in the future, then deal with them now. You may find that you are wrong, but it is much better to discover at the beginning than later on.

- Assume nothing.

Your own assumptions about yourself and your relationship may not coincide with those of your partner. Do not assume that what you want and expect out of life is automatically what they want as well. You do not know anything unless you ask. In many cases actions speak louder than words, so take a long hard look at the way you interact and do not make assumptions based entirely on past experience: every relationship is different and no two people are exactly the same.

- Be willing to adjust.

Learning to live together will take a period of adjustment for both of you. Embarking on a marriage is a new and exciting adventure. No matter what you try to plan, fate can step in at any time and we sometimes have to alter our chosen courses completely. Be willing to adjust to changes in careers and aspirations or financial upheavals and geographical movement. Most of these things will affect you at some time in your life and a willingness to adjust is vital to successful co-existence.

- Never believe it will last for ever; blind faith is dangerous.

If you believe that you are going to stay together no matter what, then it may prevent you from working on the relationship. We all change and develop as we get older and the feelings we have in our early twenties may not be the same in our thirties. So do not believe that just because you are married, everything will therefore be alright. It may well be, but not without ups and downs.

- Be prepared to put some effort in; everything of value requires it.

Following on from the last paragraph, be prepared to put some effort into maintaining your relationship. Never be complacent about your love for one another. It is a precious thing and needs to be nurtured and developed. Just being married and 'in love' is not enough. You must also be kind, prepared to listen and adjust and feel fully committed to the relationship as a basis for living your life.

- Do not be afraid to laugh. Humour can alter any situation for the better.

It is a gift to have a good sense of humour. Not all situations in life are funny, but laughter promotes an enormous feeling of well-being and is known to reduce stress levels. Apart from that, life is too short to be taken absolutely seriously all the time. Laugh together as you will cry together. Expressing your emotions and humour is one of the most life-enhancing gifts we can have. Use it and enjoy it; it can even alleviate physical pain.

Counselling

At various stages in this book, I have advised that couples or individuals seek specific forms of counselling. Who and where you choose to find counselling is up to you and depends on the availability of such services. However, if a couple feel that a friend or spiritual advisor is also suitable, then they should seek help there.

However, especially in terms of psychosexual counselling, if you are not happy with the service provided by a certain practitioner, shop around for someone else and do not let a bad experience put you off counselling altogether. It may take time to find someone that you feel you can trust and work with. But persevere, as good counselling can alleviate a whole manner of emotional problems and therefore save marriages.

ONE

Love and Expectations

It is advisable to be in love with your partner prior to marrying them. This may sound ridiculous, but not everyone who marries believes that they are genuinely 'in love' prior to the marriage. Some may think that they will grow to love the other; in reality this rarely happens and it is therefore wiser to wait until love is present between you before committing yourself fully.

Generally speaking when you fall in love, you know about it. At the very beginning, you will find yourself thinking about the other person the second you open your eyes in the morning, every few minutes throughout the day and always the last thing at night. In the initial stages of love you will not be completely aware of the other person's faults and you will feel almost 'blessed' or 'privileged' in some way to have met this wonderful example of humanity. You may find yourself being unable to eat properly and unusually anxious or nervous. You will become overtly interested in your own appearance and new clothing is usually purchased as you 'display your feathers' to your new love. These feelings are not exclusive to the very young, they can happen to anyone at any time. But be warned: you must not be tempted to marry during this phase, because it wears off!

ENGAGEMENT

A strange by-product of this feeling is a slight inability to be brutally honest about yourself, which varies from person to person. Many people have insisted to their new lover that they are terribly interested in his/her hobbies and pastimes. Hundreds of women have stood freezing to death on football terraces or joined clubs and societies in order to impress their boyfriends. Also many men have insisted they really enjoy an afternoon in the shopping mall. Once the marriage vows have been exchanged, people relax a little and true colours are shown. You cannot complain about an aspect of your partner's behaviour which you always hated but failed to mention until after the wedding. Is it any wonder that so many people complain that their partner has changed since they got married?

It is wise to have a period of engagement during which you really get a chance to discover the differences between you. If you marry during the 'terrified I'm going to lose him/her' phase, then you will find it difficult to adjust when this feeling wears off. Love is not about fear. It is about being comfortable and happy with who you are and who the other person is. I cannot offer a chronological guide as to when fear leaves and relaxation sets in – but it can take months or years. Use your engagement to get to know one another properly. Slowly reveal yourself and create the circumstances for your partner to do the same.

LUST

It is easy to confuse physical attraction with love and it is quite possible to be sexually aroused by many different people. But building a life together requires more than passion. Some women get very mixed up about love and may pretend to be 'in love' with a man rather than admit to feelings of pure lust. But both men and women need to ask themselves, at the beginning of any new relationship, if they feel they really like and admire the person they are sleeping with, or are they simply bowled over by the dizzy heights of sexual ecstasy. Couples who spend most of their courtship in bed frequently have difficulty coping later on in the marriage when bills, children and in-laws become part of the equation. Remember, love cannot live on sex alone. You may also get the impression that because you are constantly aroused by your partner now that it will always be the case. For some lucky people it will be, but for a large number sexual activity becomes less frequent after a year or two together and decreases even more after children come along.

Powerful attraction is quite difficult to define. Some people may find it happens several times in their lives; others will find one love while relatively young that will persist for a lifetime. It should not be assumed that every time deep and powerful desire is felt between two people that it alone will sustain them throughout the years ahead.

People who have had successful marriages, lasting for many years, may well have started out with a loving attraction but it then developed into mutual respect, trust and a genuine bonding of interdependency. It is respect and trust that must be cultivated right at the beginning in order for the relationship to withstand a lifetime of change, both within each partner as individuals and in the relationship as a whole.

IN LOVE WITH LOVE

Needing to be 'in love' is a dangerous situation to be in. There is incredible pressure put upon single people to be in a relationship and it can lead to feelings of terrible inadequacy. It can be difficult being unattached when all about you appear to be in couples, but try to use your 'single' time constructively. You cannot create love. It will happen when it will and although there is nothing wrong in joining a reputable introduction agency or frequenting places where single people mix, do not expect to meet the person who is going to change your life overnight.

A lot of single women complain that as they get older they feel ostracized by their friends with partners. It is wise to ignore this and concentrate on enjoying yourself, however you choose, for as long as you want. Men and women can be great friends and being single and indeed, celibate can have very positive aspects. Freedom need not necessarily spell loneliness. Marriage, mortgage and children are not suitable for everyone. Many married people wish that they had waited longer before taking on responsibilities, so enjoy your life every day, whether you are married or not. Besides, if you are too desperate to find a partner, it usually shows and is very off-putting to other people. Being married to the wrong person is a much lonelier existence than being alone.

OBSESSIVE LOVE

Obsessive love is quite rare but can occur when a person 'falls' for another and feels that they 'cannot live' without him/her. It is usually unrequited and in its extreme form can cause years of pain and trauma both for the obsessed and the object of their desire. If you persist in pursuing a lover who has told you that they cannot return your love, then you must try to seek professional help.

Some people feel that because their own feelings are so powerful they cannot be ignored and that they impart an almost God-given right to pursue their dream partner. They may imagine all manner of scenarios which become a perverse reality in their own mind. Being aware that you are obsessing is the beginning of curing it. But you do not have to do it alone: counselling is the only real way of treating this condition, so get help at once if you believe you are allowing your life to be ruled by an unrequited desire for another individual. It does not mean that you will not be able to love normally again, nor does it mean that without 'having' the other person you will be terminally unhappy. The origins of this problem lie in the background of the individual experiencing the obsession and without treatment, they may find they are unable ever to enjoy healthy, loving relationships.

Being obsessed with someone else is a very lonely feeling but it can become an addictive loneliness. Chronic lack of self-worth will help to perpetuate the obsession and prevent you from ever coming to terms with rejection. We are all of us rejected at some stage in our lives – by employers, friends, families and lovers. Being able to cope with it is part of growing up and although it is a painful process, coming through it teaches us invaluable lessons for life.

YOUTH

Very young people have a lesser chance of making a successful marriage because their emotional development is not complete, even though when they marry they may be deeply in love. The inability fully to understand the changes within themselves and in each other will hinder their chances of remaining loyal and faithful, as self-exploration has not reached a stage of happy self-love.

Co-existence requires patience, especially in the first few years as people learn to establish the ground rules and find their own space in the marital home. This does not mean that all teenage marriages are doomed to failure because it is not the case. But the chance of a successful life-long union is much diminished when the couple are very young.

HABITS

No matter how attracted you might be to someone, ask
yourself if they have any habits that irritate you. If these
bother you when you are only boyfriend/girlfriend, how
would they affect you if you were married? If you truly love
someone, they tend not to annoy you very much, certainly
not at the very beginning. But be very careful: if his/her habits
bother you, do not think you can change them and 'knock
them into shape'. If you really love someone you would not
want to change them. However, niggling habits can become
serious problems later on. For example, in the course of my
research, many people complained to me about their
partner's table manners. If you are going to be sharing meal
times with someone almost every day, it will be difficult to
ignore that person, for example, scraping their plate or talking
with an open mouth full of food. It may seem insignificant
now, but it might drive you mad later on.

WHAT MAKES US FALL IN LOVE?

Essentially we fall in love with people in whom we recognize
something of ourselves. Even couples who would appear to
have nothing in common may have a similar psychological
make-up, in terms of their background and future
expectations. This is more than enough.

Philosophers and scientists have laboured for centuries on
the reasons why love exists. However, some things are better
simply accepted than dissected. Contrary to popular belief,
we do choose who we fall in love with and this depends very
much on our attitude to ourselves. If you are happy and
secure you are unlikely to fall in love with someone who is
miserable and insecure. By the same token, it is possible to

choose to fall in love with someone who reminds you of a person who loved you earlier in your life. If you equate love with childhood images of nurturing or even abuse, you will seek the same in adult relationships. Bear in mind that if you are lonely and frightened you will not be a good judge of character. Take care of yourself first and you will want to be with people who respect you. If you believe yourself to be worthless, you will attract people who use you and you will return that attraction. If you are sad, lonely and confused, others can sense it, no matter how good you may think you are at covering it up.

BEING APART

The enormous depth of passion felt in the initial months together can appear all-encompassing and many have lost minds and lives as a direct result of the power of love. However, the initial euphoria can only continue where the couple have difficulties in being together as often as they would like.

Separation from a loved one for an uncomfortable period of time, be it days, weeks or months will lend itself to the person in love sometimes becoming ill through the need to be in the company of that one special person.

People in the initial stages of a loving affair describe an empty feeling when their lover is not with them. Unfortunately, prolonged periods apart and environmental or cultural pressures preventing the couple from having sufficient time together will serve only to enhance romantic idealism. Once together again, the memory of this romance and the hope that it will continue will make it difficult for the couple to face up to problems in their relationship when they inevitably arise.

Couples in love should never, where possible, be prevented either by family pressure or cultural differences from being together. Enforced separation will only make couples endeavour even more to find their own space. People need time to discover if their affair will become a lifelong commitment and if prevented from doing so it can embitter them to the preventing forces for the rest of their lives.

This is even more startling in the cases of very young people who fall in love. Parental pressure may make their meetings difficult, but parents who think that keeping two adolescents apart will prevent them from actually trying to see each other are painfully misguided. If there is one sure way of enhancing the passion of youth it is for elders to try to prevent it.

TIME AND PRIVACY

Therefore, no matter what your age at the beginning of the relationship, give yourselves time. This does not mean that a period of courtship should last for months or years. It means that you should spend quality time together. Time in private where you are free to get to know one another as fully and as intimately as possible.

It is only through private hours that you can discover the true depth of your feelings for each other. Time spent talking to one another, sharing important moments in your past, exchanging opinions and ideas and finding out little details about each other and therefore building trust.

Take time away from as many outside pressures as possible. This does not mean ignore family and friends. It means that when you are together with your partner, create situations where interruption is minimal and privacy guarded. This should be a time of discovery and adventure. Only through intimate conversation can bonds be formed. They do not form in the pub or cinema, but in each other's minds and that is why plenty of privacy hours are vital.

SO LET'S GET MARRIED

The patterns which form the long-term nature of the marriage are set down remarkably quickly. In a civilized culture dominance and submission should have been replaced by equal co-existence, but many people still fall into the trap in early marriage of assuming that what works for other couples must also work for them and that one individual must maintain a dominant force over the other.

This is primarily why it is important to have fully established your own identity prior to sharing your life with another individual and to maintain that sense of identity throughout your married life.

POWER

In the past, financial clout has been the power base for the marriage and as we know this was traditionally held by the male. However, in a rapidly changing world where many women are in control of their own finances, power within the marriage must be shared.

Power is not a word normally associated with happy relationships, but from the beginning of courtship it plays an important part in the success or failure of the marriage. From the beginning one or both of the parties must make decisions which will affect both of them.

As most courtship begins with the couple sharing leisure and social time, one or both of them will decide how and where that leisure time will be spent and how much revenue will be devoted to it.

Later on, as the relationship develops and the couple set up home together, decisions have to be made as to how and where they will live, whether it will depend on job opportunities for one of them and whether either of them needs to remain in close proximity with parents and existing pre-marriage friends and so forth. Therefore make a point of consulting each other about any decision that affects you both. If you choose to share your life with someone, you owe it to them and to yourself to acknowledge that responsibility and part of it means relinquishing some power which you may have taken for granted in the past; otherwise marriage will be very hard indeed.

CHOICES

The couple will therefore have to become accustomed to making all sorts of choices together. There are things which will affect both of you and major decisions must never be left to one person.

Compatibility is made easier if you both have similar attitudes to money, leisure and home environment. But no matter how much financial clout you have within the relationship, never make a major decision which will affect both your lives without full discussion with your partner, particularly when these decisions involve money or children.

If, for instance, a man decides to stop working and take up a hobby full-time, or a women decides to stop using contraception without telling her husband, difficulties are bound to ensue. When we get married, our separate needs have to be taken into account but must also be looked at within the framework of the marriage, that is if we want the marriage to work.

Do not assume that because you love living in a remote

farmhouse that your suburban partner is also going to love it. Remember, you are individuals and even though you may be the most compatible couple ever, you are still bound to have differing likes and dislikes.

GIVING IN

Younger women still tend to let major decisions be made by their partner. However, after a few years of marriage and maturity, it can be difficult to let all the decisions affecting your life be made by someone else, even if you love that person. Resentment may build up when a woman feels she is not being fully consulted in major decision-making.

But some women can be their own worst enemies. It does feel good to have a dependable and reliable person to lean on occasionally, but some pretend to be incapable of making decisions because they are frightened that their husband will then lean on them too much or because they want to remain little girls in the bodies of women.

This can be carried on quite successfully in the early years of marriage, but it is hard to pretend to be a helpless princess when you are a thirty-year-old married woman with two children and a mortgage.

Men do not want to be married to doormats. A confident woman is always more desirable. However, if either of you insists on being 'the boss' or 'ruling the roost' perhaps you should ask yourself whether marriage is a good idea at all.

Learn to talk together about all the major decisions you have to make. Do not assume that you know what is best for your partner: think first about what is best for you and then start talking. Compromise is necessary, but not unconditional surrender. Both should learn to think through their own needs and make choices which suit them both.

ROWS

Do not accept the age-old belief that rows are wrong. Two people who see each other almost every day have got to disagree. It is quite impossible to expect to go through married life without rows and arguments. They happen and in a healthy relationship, the couple get a chance during an argument to say things to each other which are better said than left to rot inside. We all exaggerate our partner's faults when we have a row and frequently we say things which we do not mean. But no one is perfect and it is especially important for young women – who are in the main terrified of arguments – to realize that they do not have to be kind, forgiving and compassionate all the time.

Arguments do not have to be destructive and painful. In fact they can be passionate and enhance that sense of freedom to be yourself which makes a good marriage work. A short row is far better than built-up tension, which can be really dangerous.

Say nothing at your peril. This does not mean that you should be at each other's throats all the time, but you should not be frightened to say what you feel as short rows tend to fire up quickly and then disappear and may ultimately draw you closer together.

HUMOUR

In a world where there are constant reminders of pain and suffering and where most of us live under a particular level of stress, humour can be the one thing that saves us from really hurting ourselves.

Some scenarios are genuinely not funny, but very few. Having a sense of humour helps you view life and yourself in a kinder way and can really sustain your marriage if you allow it to.

Some people are born with a natural ability not to take life too seriously. They are not necessarily comedians and may not even come across as being funny characters, but they have an in-built ability to approach life in a particular way. Even if you are not possessed of these powers, learn to look at the funny side sometimes. You do not have to be serious all your life, nor do you have to feign sorrow because you are expected to. There is enough genuine pain without pretending it exists when it does not. Even if you want to wallow in sadness, try laughing instead: remember, your partner may not always appreciate your misery.

5 GOOD REASONS NOT TO GET MARRIED

1. Because you want to increase your status in society.

   It is true that an enormous pressure is put upon people to be part of a couple. However, although this may appear difficult to resist, do not let it tempt you into marriage. Try not to let your decisions be swayed by social intervention, or to marry just because you think you will be more respected in the world. Respect is something that has to be earned, not a 'free gift' that comes with the marriage certificate.

2. Because you are getting 'older' and think you are running out of time.

   Ignore ageism, especially from older relatives who are typically bad at giving advice. Do not concern yourself with fears of being inadequate just because you are not married and are reaching an age when most people are. Marry when and if you feel like it, not because you are pushing thirty and developing paranoia.

3. You want children.

   This alone is not a good enough reason for getting married. Children should be the product of a healthy, happy relationship. Some women get terrified that their 'biological clock' is ticking away and although there is some evidence to suggest that there are increased health risks for older pregnant women, a lot depends on the general health of the individual, irrespective of her age. Besides, you do not have physically to give birth in order to raise a family: there are thousands of children in local authority care, who are already in need of parents.

4. You have met someone whom you do not want anyone else to have.

   If you believe that by manipulating someone into marrying you then you are going to have them all to yourself, you are badly misguided and dangerously lacking in self-worth. Marriage is a partnership between two people who wish legally and emotionally to bind their union. However, it is not ownership. One person never, ever owns another and should not desire to. Marriages based on this lack of security in one or both partners has no chance of survival. If you truly love someone, let them be free to make their own decisions. If they truly love you they will want to be with you. You cannot create desire. It just happens.

5. You are already pregnant and want to 'legitimize' the child.

   Pregnancy can sometimes force people into making a premature decision to marry. It does not guarantee that you will both be happy and fulfilled and that having a baby together will seal your relationship. You can call your baby, legally, any name you desire and society no longer frowns upon children whose parents are not married. Let your relationship develop in spite of the child, not because of it. Babies are made by a sexual liaison and not always between people who genuinely love and care for one another.

In an ideal world, children are raised by two caring adults, usually the parents, but the person with whom you are about to share parenthood may not necessarily be the person with whom you want to spend the rest of your life.

EXPECTATIONS

Unrealistic expectations can be very dangerous in the planning and preparation of the impending marriage. It is surprising how many couples have quite differing expectations of how the marriage will 'turn out' and many people find that the married state does not live up to their expectations of it.

Even those who did not come from particularly happy home environments themselves still expect their own marriages to be better and/or different from that of their parents. However we tend to carry with us unrealistic expectations of relationships in general and particularly of marriage.

People change and the young couple in their twenties may be quite different to the same couple in the thirty- and then forty-something category.

Older married people, particularly parents, are not always honest with their adult children when it comes to warning them of the pitfalls in a realistic way. This is because they are ashamed to admit that they have not always found marriage to be easy and, mistakenly, do not want to blight their offspring's view of it.

However, honest advice from older relatives can be helpful,

if you can find one who is prepared to tell you the whole truth and nothing but. We cannot expect our relationship to be like any other but advice given correctly and without selfishness can be helpful.

Endeavour, therefore, to have realistic expectations of marriage. None of the clichés truly apply. If you want to avoid heart-breaking disappointment, talk to each other about how you both expect the relationship to develop. There needs to be a healthy balance between cynicism and romance.

MISCONCEPTIONS

There are several main misconceptions which ought to be considered.

- Neither of you will ever be attracted to anyone else.

  You will both at some stage or other and to varying levels be attracted to someone other than your spouse. Being aware that this is part of being human can help you cope with it when it occurs, which it inevitably will. However, this does not mean that this attraction should be acted upon, but neither assume that after you marry the rest of the world stops existing and that marriage will blind you to the beauty of others. In some cases it can increase your awareness of the power of sexual attraction.
- You will always be friends.

  You won't. Any relationship which involves daily contact over a long period of time will lend itself to disagreements. Most people find that friendships happen by accident and like love, develop over years. Good friends need to have periods apart from one another in order for the friendship to be sustained. You cannot expect to be always 'friendly' with someone whom you see every day. Expect to fall out with each other occasionally and don't panic if you get fed up with each other's company: it doesn't spell the end of your marriage.

- You will never be bored.

You will. Life can be tedious for everyone. If you had periods of boredom before you were married, you will still have them afterwards. It is important not to resent your partner when you are bored. You would probably be bored anyway. However, if the boredom intensifies, do something about it. Change your routine and try something new and don't blame your partner if you are bored all the time. It's not up to them to entertain you.

- You should do everything together.

Never attempt this. Remember you are individuals, above all else. Maintaining separate interests, and sometimes friends, is vital. Do not try and be interested in absolutely everything your partner does. If you hate fishing, shopping, football, soap opera, etc. say so. Let your partner be free to enjoy what they do, as long as it doesn't separate you to the point of resentment, or impinge unduly upon household income.

- Having children will bring you closer together.

This is the biggest fallacy of all. Having a baby is one of the most stressful events in the life of any human being. If you are having serious problems in your relationship, do not attempt to resolve them by having children. It will serve only to keep you busier for a few years and reduce the amount of time you spend together, but it will not necessarily improve your marriage. Sort out your problems with each other before introducing another person into them. It is selfish in the extreme to bring a child into an unhappy home by choice. Think of the child, before yourself.

SUMMARY

- Learn to discuss small decisions and it will be easier to share larger ones.
- Do not assume you know what your partner is thinking. Ask their opinion.
- Bear in mind the social needs of your partner. A happy marriage needs outward stimulation for both partners.
- Don't lie to please. Be honest or you will regret it.
- Don't have children to 'make things better'. It won't.

TWO

Weddings

A wedding is a celebration to mark the formal recognition of a couple's choice to spend the rest of their lives together.

Traditional white weddings are not always the best way to begin married life. They remain enormously popular, but the size and expense of the wedding bears no relation to the success of the marriage. Most women see this as the only day in their lives when they get the opportunity to look like a character from a fairy tale, to be as beautiful as they can possibly be and also to be the centre of attention within the family unit - and this is exactly where the danger can lie.

Most little girls dream of their wedding day. We all want to be Cinderella or Sleeping Beauty. Men think about the envy of their friends when they see them leaving the church with a beautiful princess on their arm. Couples can sometimes spend years planning and preparing for the day itself and weddings are seen in Western society as one of the biggest excuses for families to celebrate and enjoy themselves.

A traditional wedding is, in fact, a large party. Few modern couples regularly attend church or give thought to the spiritual aspect of their wedding, but church weddings are considered the best way to begin married life.

I stress that large church weddings are not a bad thing, if it is what the couple genuinely want and can afford. But in the months prior to the ceremony, people can become so involved with the preparation for this alone, that they forget about planning for after the wedding, which is when the marriage really begins.

Some people realize, after all the preparations have been made, that they do not want to marry but are too frightened to cancel the wedding. The fear of 'letting down' parents and friends can make them go through with the wedding although they are having second thoughts about the marriage itself. If voiced, these fears are explained as 'pre-wedding nerves', not pre- marriage fears, which is what they are.

In our early twenties, which is when most people marry, romanticism still plays a large part in the desire to have a traditional wedding. A young couple know that, once engaged, they are the centre of attention within the family and everyone gets involved in the preparation for the wedding, especially the parents of the bride. This is not always a good thing. Many brides have had the wedding their mothers arranged for them and not the wedding of their choice.

In recent years the increased popularity of package holidays comprising a marriage ceremony on a foreign beach is an indication of how far some couples will go to avoid family pressure on their wedding day. However, these weddings tend to be chosen by older couples, who are not dependent on their parents making a financial contribution towards the day.

Some people describe a feeling of deflation in the weeks after the wedding. This is because the preparations for it have filled so much of their time that they find themselves feeling slightly empty and almost wishing they could begin planning their wedding all over again. All couples want to have a day which they can enjoy and cherish the memory of, but a traditional wedding is not always the best way to do it. In the flurry over the dress, cake, church, etc. couples tend to forget that what they are actually doing is making a public statement of their love for each other and their decision to remain lifelong partners.

How a wedding is held should be to the complete choice of the couple themselves. Families tend to be hurt if the couple do not always agree with them as to how they make their vows, but the marriage has nothing to do with our parents or relatives. The marriage is about the two people getting married and no one else. Young couples should never be pressurized into having any kind of ceremony which they do not want and brides especially should think very seriously about why they may want a traditional wedding. Is it the wedding they want and not the marriage? Is it to please relatives? Is it because they feel it is expected of them? Do they think that a large white wedding will seal their marriage vows?

In planning a wedding of any kind, whether church, registry office or on a beach in the Caribbean, remember these points.

- The marriage is more important than the wedding.

  The wedding lasts for a couple of hours. The marriage should be for life. It is about building a life with someone, and this should always be at the forefront of the couple's choice.

- Parental approval does not guarantee a long and happy marriage.

  This can cloud all sorts of issues. Everyone wants and needs the love and approval of their family, but pleasing them will not make marriages work. The day is for the couple and no one else.

- Attention spans are shorter than we think.

  We all want to be the centre of attention at some stage in our lives, but making grand statements can be dangerous. Remember that after one day, the wedding becomes a memory and a box of photographs. No matter how much you want to be seen by the world at your best, there are other ways of doing it.

- Weddings do not have to be expensive to be good.

  The hardest way to begin married life is with even minor financial problems. No matter how much you want an expensive dress and a huge reception, these things do not necessarily make the wedding a success. Concentrate more on the guest list. Any successful party is dependent upon who is there and not how much it cost.

- Above all else, please yourselves.

  By all means treat your family to a good day out if you want, but it is your day, to be spent as you both desire. You are beginning a whole new life and that is what must be taken into account. You must want to enjoy it and if that means a small informal gathering or an enormous affair, so be it. It will only be yours to treasure.

THE HONEYMOON

What is a honeymoon?

Very few couples now wait until after marriage to begin a sexual relationship, although some do. Previously the honeymoon was a period of rest away from family and friends designed to give the couple time to relax and explore their new sexual relationship, in the immediate days after their wedding.

As more couples now live together before getting married, or at least have experienced some form of sexual liaison, the honeymoon is now considered a holiday and nothing more.

If you and your partner have never been on holiday together before, it is advisable that you do so before going away for the first time in the days after the wedding. Holidays, especially those taken abroad, can be more stressful than we are sometimes willing to admit.

We can become quite different people when we are away from our natural environment. Being in a foreign setting gives us a new-found freedom and a chance to do things which we would not normally do at home. There are certain important factors to be considered when planning a honeymoon. Many couples leave the decision as to where to go to the husband, who may arrange a trip to a surprise destination, but his choice of a relaxing holiday may not be hers and vice versa.

You must discuss together what your ideal of a holiday is. Not everyone enjoys visiting hot countries and lying on beaches. I for one can think of nothing worse. While you are still engaged, it is better to plan a short break together before getting married. This can be a valuable lesson in companionship. Away from family and friends you may discover new sides to each other which you didn't realize existed.

If one of you enjoys visiting museums and art galleries and the other likes to scuba dive all day, choose a destination which can cater to both your tastes. If you are nervous about long-distance travel, do not be frightened to admit it; and if you are worried about visiting a country where you would have trouble being understood or where you know your eating habits would simply not be catered for, you should make your feelings known.

A honeymoon, like any other holiday, should be spent in a place where rest and relaxation are paramount. You will need privacy and time alone together. It is inadvisable to visit a country where one of you has visited with a previous lover and where memories may cloud the trip.

Have a good look at your various holiday ideas and reach a compromise. Many couples have discovered quite disturbing personality conflicts whilst on holiday. It is possible that we are only our true selves when we are freed from work and family ties and it is better to discover this before we get married.

Challenge the idea of a foreign holiday for a honeymoon. It is true that you will both need to spend some time together in private, but going abroad is not always the best place to do this. A few days in a small hotel in your own country can be just as romantic and a lot less stressful than two weeks abroad. You need to concentrate on being together and resting after the wedding. Coping with a foreign language, currency, extremes of climate and unusual food is not always relaxing. If you are both seasoned travellers then so be it. However, if you are a novice to foreign travel, it can be best explored later in the marriage rather than at the very beginning.

What you need is to be in a place that will give you both the ultimate opportunity to relax, walk, make love, eat together and generally wind down. These are the considerations when choosing a honeymoon. Do not be concerned about where your friends have recently been on holiday: you are not in competition with anyone else. It is a precious time to be remembered by both of you and hopefully revisited later in the marriage.

So, before you book anything, consider these points:

- Try to take a holiday together before the wedding.
  It need not be an expensive trip, but somewhere removed from your home environment. You will learn a lot about each other, especially if it is your first time together in an alien environment. Do not wait to go on honeymoon before discovering something awful about your partner.
- Ask yourself what your ideal way of relaxing is.
  You may have very different opinions. Be honest about your needs. What is relaxing for one may be hell to another.
- Think carefully about going abroad.

If it is a new experience it may prove more stressful then you need. Look at resorts in your own country. It will always have much to offer. A beautiful hotel in the depths of your native countryside can be infinitely more romantic than a half-built resort on the Costa del Sol.

- Remember you will be pretty tired after the wedding.

Rest is vital. Choose a trip without too much travelling. You want to come back refreshed and relaxed. If you can afford first class all the way, so be it, but travelling on a tight budget is not as romantic as it might appear.

- Romance is the key to a successful honeymoon.

Some places are more romantic than others. Choose a resort that is likely to be peaceful and allow you both time and privacy.

- Do not overspend on the honeymoon.

The amount you spend does not always guarantee an enjoyable vacation. It is better to have a few days spent together in a small resort than to waste money travelling far away, just because it is your honeymoon.

- You will both appreciate a holiday six to eight months after the wedding.

A honeymoon does not necessarily have to be taken in the two weeks immediately afterwards. A honeymoon can be spent at any time, in any place.

- The first few days of married life are a precious time.

They can feel strange and you both will need time to adjust to your new found status. Bear this in mind when choosing your honeymoon destination.

- Do not try to compete with other people's holidays.

This is a special time for both of you to be enjoyed as you both desire. We all have different conceptions of relaxation and friends may not always be honest about their experiences.

- Try to talk to someone who has visited the destination that you have chosen.

  If you have decided to go abroad, do not be shy of inquiring from your tour operator exactly what you can expect when you get there. Explain that you will be on honeymoon and pay particular attention to the other people who are likely to be holidaying there at the same time. You do not want an expensive trip ruined by noise, crowds and confusion.

SUMMARY

- The size and expense of the wedding bears no relation to the success of the marriage.
- A traditional wedding is a large party which lasts for one day only.
- Avoid over-spending on the wedding, if it means starting your married life in debt; maintain a realistic budget.
- Do not ignore pre-wedding nerves: they may be genuine pre-marriage fears.
- Do not let the wedding preparations become more important than the marriage vows.
- Have the wedding you want and not the wedding your family expects. It is for you and your partner to be enjoyed as you both wish.
- If possible pay for as much of the celebrations as you can yourself: it gives you more control over the arrangements.
- Parental approval does not guarantee a long and happy marriage.

- A honeymoon is a holiday which can be taken at any time.
- Think carefully about your honeymoon destination. Foreign travel, especially for the uninitiated, can be extremely stressful.
- Try to have some form of break away from home together before your honeymoon. It can be a real eye-opener.

THREE

Role Playing

According to statistical evidence most of us marry for the first time in our twenties, with the female usually being younger than the male. Then, some time later, over 70 per cent of divorce petitions will be sought by the young blushing bride of previous years. A lot of us have now fallen into that particular pattern - so what makes most of us marry so young only to abandon our marriages later on?

THE FOLLOWING SECTION IS INTENDED FOR WOMEN

Adopting a Role

It is very easy for women to adopt a certain role in early marriage and then discover that they can't keep it up. A newly married woman will frequently adopt the role of carer and therefore set that pattern for the marriage. We adopt this role primarily out of fear. We have been conditioned to look after men and that is usually what we do. But we do not have to. Not every man wants to be treated like a child and trying to be his mother will not make him love you more, nor stop him from treating you badly, if he so chooses.

Most men enjoy the early years of marriage and women find them difficult. This is because women are frightened to admit, for example, that housework is boring, that they want to get promotion at work, that they really do hate cooking

and that they are not that interested in their partner's day.
Few will admit this, however, and unfortunately the vast
majority of home care is still carried out by women,
irrespective of whether or not they work outside the home
or are full-time housekeepers.

The problem with adopting a role is that it is generally
copied from someone else, usually our own mothers.
Unfortunately we cannot expect that role model to work for
us because we are usually better informed than our parents,
yet we persist in trying to be nurturers to our new husbands
as we mistakenly believe that it is what will keep them happy
and make the marriage work. Wrong!

If role playing can be adapted according to the changes life
brings, then the relationship will survive, albeit on a false
premise. However, there are marriages that have lasted for
years which are based entirely on the female adopting a role
from which she then finds it impossible to escape. Young
women today are less stoical than their older female relatives
and due to increased awareness are less likely to continue role
playing after discovering it to be an impossible mode of living.

Housework

There must be few people, men or women, who genuinely
find house care fulfilling. A clean environment is necessary
to survival, however, and someone must take care of it.

We all have different standards of cleanliness. What to some
people is a priority, to others is unnecessary. How many
people are naturally good cooks or find pleasure in the
buying, preparation and serving of meals? The point is to be
honest, not just with your partner but with yourself. If you
do enjoy certain aspects of home care then take responsibility
for the those. If however there are certain things which make
you unhappy, don't do them. If you hate to iron clothes, then

don't iron them. If you hate to cook, don't cook. No man will ever starve. He lived well before he met you and he is not about to shrivel up and die because the kitchen is your least favourite room in the house. It does not make you a failure. Remember, you are not his mother. He may already have one of those and one is enough.

Guilt

Do not let guilt stop you from being honest with a new partner. Don't try and sell yourself to him as an 'all singing, all dancing' Wonderwoman. If that is what he wants he is better staying with his family. Don't be frightened that he will not love you if he discovers that you are a terrible cook and you don't know one end of a vacuum cleaner from the other. You do not expect him to be a natural housekeeper so why on earth should he expect that of you?

Do not consider yourself lucky to have got him. You should never think along those lines: while you keep him on a pedestal you are never going to be honest with him, nor he with you. You are not his other half, or her indoors, or the missus, or whatever he may choose to call you; you are an individual. You are not lucky to have each other, you have simply fallen in love and are feeling lucky. There is a difference. If you continue to always consider him to be the most important person in the world, you will feel guilty to admit to any kind of negative emotion, such as sadness, loneliness or depression. You will, of course, feel all these things at some stage in your life, to varying degrees, but guilt will prevent you from voicing them and that is very damaging indeed.

Worship

Remember that love is not hero worship. It is about caring, honesty, freedom, companionship and togetherness. You may love him dearly but he is a human being and even the best of them cannot live up to worship for very long.

In your first few months together try to be honest with him. If he upsets or annoys you then talk to him about it. Resentments kept inside are like small tumours. They can eat away at you for years and then become suddenly fatal. Get rid of them when they arise and never be ashamed of having them. If you want to keep him, be yourself and be honest. Try not to look at him for the fulfilment of all your hopes and dreams. Only you can provide that for yourself. Other people can help to enhance your happiness but they do not create it.

Sharing

In an ideal world home chores would be equally shared. However, no one wants to empty the litter tray and women are more likely to expect a clean and tidy environment and are therefore more likely to do housework. This is a big part of our social programming. It can be so subtle that we are not even aware of it. Therefore, it is important to try to eliminate guilt from your attitude to housework. No-one will judge you more harshly than you judge yourself. Be kind to yourself and he will follow suit. Ask him to help you. Do not encourage him to be helpless. Later on in your married life, especially if and when you have children, you are going to have to work together. So put your shoulders back, smile sweetly and hand him the vacuum cleaner.

Other Women

Other women play a major role in our attitudes to house care, food preparation and even motherhood. Competition from other women is never far from the mind of the newly married. Sometimes it is the fear of the reaction of other women which drives us to seek perfection in our home life. Few women want to admit that they are having difficulties in adjusting to their new lifestyle and the garbled advice from older female relatives can sometimes increase fears instead of removing them.

Be strong in your attitude to other women. How they run their lives is their business. What you are searching for is a set-up which suits you and your partner. If others do not always agree with your chosen methods it is not your problem. Early marriage is a time of discovery and that time is too precious to be spent worrying unnecessarily about other people. You have just made a huge choice: to decide to marry is to make an adult decision. You no longer need the gossip of the school yard. It is your life to be enjoyed. Let other women iron their aprons if they so wish; it is up to them.

Leaving Home

Loneliness is not something that is normally associated with the beginning of married life. However, when young couples start out in a new environment, some women find that they miss their family and pre-marriage friends. Working helps to alleviate this, but for women who do not work spending time at home all day, especially if a baby is present, can appear to be the loneliest time of their lives.

As more people move away from the place where they grew up and settle in new cities with their partners, the strain of forming new friendships can make the marriage seem oppressive. One person cannot replace a whole network of friends and relatives. As long as couples realize this and make as much preparation as they can beforehand to ease this adjustment, the new move can become an exciting adventure for you both to enjoy.

A busy partner may not always understand, but women must remember not to feel guilty or unappreciative just because they are not instantly happy the second the rings are exchanged. They should be prepared for feelings of loneliness. Separation from family is always traumatic as the bride realizes that she is now at the beginning of forming a new family of her own.

If you choose to move away from family and friends, do not expect the transition to be an easy one. Sentimentality may make far-off places and old friends appear more romantic in memory than reality, however. A healthy reliance on each other and mutual support are important and form the rock on which you will build your marriage.

Establish the Ground Rules

There are no rules for success, but honesty is useful and can be employed as with any other emotional tool. Some women are lucky in that they choose to marry genuinely kind men who will share house care because they are helpful people and it is in their nature to do so. However, most men will gladly slip into the traditional male role of non-intervention in household duties and so female drudgery becomes the norm. Follow these basic rules from the start to avoid getting into destructive role play.

SUMMARY

- Be honest.

  Tell your partner, before you marry, that you do not intend to take full responsibility for house care, cooking and budgeting. This is even more important if you both work outside the home.

- Do not compare your married existence with that of any other female.

  You are an individual and you are free to choose how you organize your life.

- Do not idolize him.

  Love is not worship and you didn't get married to play master and slave.

- Do not expect your husband to be automatically helpful.

  If he is new to house care himself, he will also need time to adjust.

- Do not patronize him.

  Anyone can prepare a meal and clean a room. In fact, heavier jobs such as vacuuming are easier for him to do than you, and he'll probably do them more quickly than you would.

- Do not accept refusal.

  If he refuses to do his fair share of home care, either don't marry him, or use his wages to employ a cleaner.

- Look at your own ambitions and capabilities.

  There is nothing stopping any woman getting the career she wants and needs, with perseverance and hard work. Talk to your husband about your long-term aims and try to be as honest as possible.

- Do not accept a standard of behaviour in him
  which he would not accept in you.

  If he insists, for instance, on seeing his friends
  and socializing as much as when he was single,
  then do the same. Tell him how you feel, without
  losing your temper – if possible.
- Do not build your whole life around him.

  No matter how much you love him, hold on to
  your own dreams and aims. You can talk to him
  about these things, but make sure you never lose
  sight of them.
- Do not expect him to be the sole provider of
  your happiness.

  Happiness comes from within – his presence
  should always enhance that, not create it.
- If you are moving to a new town, be prepared to
  feel lonely at the beginning.

  Work together on this. Involve yourselves
  making new friendships, both as a couple and as
  individuals.

THE FOLLOWING SECTION IS INTENDED FOR MEN

Adopting a Role

It is not just women who start to adopt roles at the beginning
of the relationship. Men are equally capable of following the
lead of male relatives and friends and not always with happy
consequences. The unfortunate facts of divorce are that the
vast majority are petitioned by women. The seasoned married
woman of 30 will be quite a different person from the shy,
insecure young bride of 24. Women do tend to alter after the

first few years of marriage. They become much more self-assured, as if the realization of something has suddenly dawned on them. They also accept responsibility more easily and are better at setting up support systems of friends and neighbours to guard against loneliness.

The days have long gone when a woman will stay in a bad relationship just because she is married. Easier divorce and economic assistance from the government, albeit small, means that women are no longer dependent on their husbands for their economic survival or in the raising of their children. There is no longer a social stigma attached to people who are divorced, as there was in previous generations, and as a result of these social and economic changes women are actually leaving their marriages in their thousands and taking their children with them.

Most women are better educated, informed and aware than they have ever been before. They are in control of their bodies and their reproductive systems. However, they may not become aware of this until their late twenties, when they may have already been married for some time and are thoroughly fed up with the whole set up. This is not a sexist statement and there are some extremely confident people, both male and female, who are aware of all their attributes while still quite young. However, in the main, young women do not feel that they have power and freedom to live their lives as they choose. This does change with maturity and experience.

If you do not want to lose your wife, then think carefully about the role you are taking on. Remember that she will change and grow in the first few years you are together. How you treat her right at the beginning is the key in preventing her leaving you. Do not be under the impression that her dogged devotion will last forever. She may adore you now but adoration is hard to perpetuate and is much better replaced by respect.

Being a husband is quite different to being a boyfriend or even to a lesser degree a co-habitee. Despite the fact that men usually enjoy early marriage more than their wives, they must not blind themselves to the responsibility they are taking on.

Men do not always find it easy to admit to their own insecurities and failings; it is much easier for women to be honest with friends and relatives about pain and insecurity. Our society has made it very difficult for men to express their anxieties. Men are conditioned from birth not to show their feelings and are discouraged from crying. They are sometimes treated more harshly and expected to cope better with the rigours of growing up.

This can lead to an enormous build-up of tension and frustration in men. A lot of them are under the impression that women expect them to be strong all the time and to hold back on their fears about life in general. The truth is that what women really want is an honest partner. Modern life is difficult and stressful at the best of times and it is important in the early stages of your relationship to try to tell your partner what you are truly feeling. Most women complain that their partner does not open up enough with them and that they frequently feel left out of his life by his reticence to talk about himself, his hopes, dreams, fears and anxieties.

Talk

If you want your marriage to thrive and grow, then talk to her. At the very beginning, learn to feel free to express yourself fully. It helps her to understand you and it will encourage her to respect you as an individual. Do not interpret silence as a show of strength. An unwillingness to open up is actually a sign of weakness and will only lend itself to further feelings of anger and resentment. 'He will not talk to me' is the most common complaint that women have when discussing their partners. It may not be easy for you to express your true feelings when you have been conditioned for years to suppress them. But most women love intimacy. They want to feel that you trust them with your innermost fears and dreams and keeping these things to yourself will be interpreted by her as you 'shutting her out'. This can cause terrible pain and loneliness for you both.

Fear

Do not be ashamed to admit to fear. We all feel it and the best way to alleviate it is to discuss it with someone you love and trust. Fears about work, performance, sexual prowess, appearance, etc. are common to everyone. Expressing them through conversation will automatically reduce them. If you begin this early in your relationship, you will become accustomed to speaking to her like this for the rest of your married life and she will respect and love you more as a result. There is nothing to fear but fear itself and our minds are quite capable of exaggerating small fears and making them enormous. However, if you are finding that anxiety is causing you daily distress, then seek professional counselling. Under no circumstances keep fears and anxieties to yourself, for they can become damaging and destructive.

Other Men

Do not look to other men for role models. Just because your father never did housework or your friends sort out their problems in the pub, it does not mean that you have to do the same. Remember that you are setting your own patterns for living. Other men may have different ways of living their lives, but it does not always make for happiness and fulfilment.

While all about you are having affairs or spending their leisure time drinking beer, it does not give you carte blanche to do the same. Just because something is socially acceptable does not always make it the right thing to do. If you love and respect your wife, then learn to trust her, and although your friendships with other men are important, do not let them impinge on your relationship with your wife - that is, if you want to keep her.

Housework

You may find that your new wife has adopted a role of carer and housekeeper and that may suit you very well. However, take into account the fact that she may not always want to do all the housework or even the vast majority, but she may not always say so, because of her own fear of failure. Therefore, try to imagine the day from her point of view. A good experiment is to swap roles for a day. From the minute you wake until the minute you fall asleep, behave exactly as your partner does; pretend to be each other. It is surprising what you can learn from this, if you are prepared to take it seriously.

Traditional female 'jobs', such as cooking, can be a marvellous mode of relaxation for anyone, men or women, when they give themselves a chance to try it. Most of the top chefs in the world are men and yet women traditionally do the cooking at home. I have actually heard men say that they 'can't cook'. Whereas *anyone* who can read a recipe book can prepare a meal. Anyone. Do not pretend that you are incapable of carrying out household chores when you know that you are more than capable. Remember that she gets tired as well, especially if she has a job outside the home.

Some men are in the habit of developing learned helplessness. This is a state that comes about when they convince themselves that they are genuinely incapable of performing any kind of household duty and may sometimes show an almost child-like dependence on their wives 'doing things for them'. They boast about having never been to a supermarket or their inability to prepare food or use a washing machine. Unfortunately some women encourage learned helplessness in their partners because of their own insecurity and so the pattern is formed. This is simply pathetic.

There is no place for this kind of behaviour in relationships today. Our grandparents may have felt chained to the norm but not so with this generation. Young women have a tendency to be everything for their partners, but the truth is that they eventually grow out of it and after a couple of years of marriage are deeply resentful of the fact that they married lazy men. To a certain extent they create their own monsters, but men seem happy to comply with this. If you want to make your marriage work, take half of the responsibility of house care and food preparation. Even if she tries to do everything for you, don't let her. Remember that once this pattern is formed it is hard to break and you may find yourself in later years with a bitter, resentful, complaining wife.

Pleasing Her

Men are sometimes strangely misguided as to how to please a woman and I do not mean sexually. There are ways in which you can make her genuinely happy and content and therefore improve both your lifestyles. Tenderness has an enormous part to play in the successful marriage.

Both of you have to be aware of the need for tenderness in your lives and women generally are. But men sometimes leave touch and affection for the bedroom when there are many other ways of expressing it and really improving your marriage.

What she really wants from you is kisses and hugs. Get into the habit of holding her and stroking her non-sexually on a daily basis. Compliment her appearance and be judicious with criticism of her. Most women feel that the world is already a highly competitive place and home should be an environment of solace and comfort. If you are watching television, hold her hand. If she has had a difficult day, offer to give her a back rub. This is what women really want. However, if she thinks that every time you touch her you are expecting sex, she will be loath to respond, especially if she is tired. Therefore, reassure her that you are being affectionate simply because you love her and not because you have any other motivation.

Tenderness costs nothing and will mean more to her than all the flowers and chocolates you can buy. Tell her that you love her when she least expects you to and show her with respect and admiration.

SUMMARY

- Do not be afraid to admit to insecurity and fear.
  Every single one of us has more or less the
  same feelings. You are not alone. A strong man is
  aware of his weaknesses.
- Do not expect your wife to treat you as your
  mother would.
  She is an individual. You should not marry her
  to have the benefits of home life with sex thrown
  in. You are entering a partnership.
- Do not try to follow bad role models.
  Whatever way your father and friends treat their

wives, is up to them. You treat yours the way that she deserves, as a human being.

- Employ tenderness in every aspect of your relationship.

  It is what she truly needs and desires.
- Respect your own anger and frustration and talk to her about it.

  If you hate your boss, do not attempt to be cruel to your wife. She will always support you if you learn to express your feelings properly.
- Do not be too proud to take on a 50:50 role in household duties, and do not be ashamed to admit when you are nervous or unsure about doing it.

  Set a healthy pattern early on and do not begrudge the time you spend cleaning and cooking.
- Remind her daily that you love her.

  She will always need to hear you saying it.
- Even if you find other women attractive, do not make comparisons.

  A bed for the night is easy. A partner for life is precious.
- Do not expect her always to want you.

  It does not mean that she has necessarily stopped loving you, but she needs a little space occasionally.
- Do not be frightened of letting her express herself in the way she dresses and presents herself.

  If you think she is wonderful, other people will as well. Be proud of her and glad that she's with you.

FOUR

Money and Careers

MONEY

No relationship can survive under the omnipresent threat of financial insecurity. This has nothing to do with the amount of revenue generated by the individuals, but their own personal perception of the kind of lifestyle they want.

Being rich or poor is relative to the couple involved and therefore financial insecurity enters when that which the individual considers a comfortable standard of living is threatened. When financial insecurity concerns you more than any other aspect of your life it is very difficult to co-exist happily.

Some people are perfectly content with a small house and a regular income for all of their lives. Others aim for bigger and 'better' things and are not happy unless they can envisage a future filled with luxury. We all have different needs but the important point is that you both agree on what you believe to be acceptable.

Fortunes can alter and change, sometimes with dramatic consequences. What once were considered 'safe' career options no longer are. Arguments over who spends what and how, are going to be the most venomous you are likely to have (apart from those concerning sex and fidelity).

How do you avoid letting financial insecurity destroy your marriage?

- Discuss standards.

  Set the parameters of a standard of living which is acceptable to you both, prior to getting married. Thrash out your opinions and don't be frightened to admit how important or unimportant money is in your life. Everybody has different ideas as to what is an acceptable lifestyle. Some are happy with a small and regular income. Others like to aim for great heights and risk all in the run-up. It does not matter as long as you both agree.

- Look at extremes.

  Discuss how extreme poverty – or extreme wealth – would be likely to affect the relationship. Pools winners do not always adjust well to new-found wealth; increased income can be as stressful as decreased income. Find out from each other what you would do with a sudden large income. It does happen and marriages do not always survive new wealth.

- Ask yourself how you feel.

  Examine your own attitude to money. Ask yourself how much responsibility towards household revenue you intend to take. Do you envisage a time in later life when that responsibility will lessen or deepen or, in other words, do you intend either to reduce or stop a personal financial contribution or to increase and build on existing income?

- Respect it.

  Learn to respect money and to love it. This does not mean seek to always have more, it means to love it for what it is, an essential part of human life. Even in its crudest form it can distort and eventually destroy the strongest of loving bonds. To ignore its importance is to deny an inner desire for security and survival.

- Talk about it.

Learn to talk about every aspect of your finances. Unfortunately pretending not to care for it or to be fearful of its power within the relationship can eventually lead to a total inability to cope without it. It plays a significant role in the survival of a marriage and problems surrounding it should be anticipated prior to their occurrence. Adequate preparation and lack of fear regarding money will enable prosperous times to be enjoyed and hard times to be dealt with realistically, sometimes drawing a couple closer together rather than tearing them apart.

- Prioritize yourself.

One or both of you may have an expensive hobby or pastime which is an integral part of your life. However, if one of you intends to use up vital family resources on a hobby which cannot be shared by the other, he or she must take into account that their partner has justification in asking them to stop.

For some people sports and activities are necessary for the alleviation of stress, however, if your partner is resentful of your hobby and the amount of money that you spend on it, then consider reducing the expenditure, at least until your financial situation has improved.

If necessary, ask yourself if you are prepared to give up a cherished pastime for the sake of a happy equilibrium at home. If you do not, don't be surprised if it leads to rows. Few women understand the lure of the golf course and few men understand the pleasure of the shopping mall; but compromises can be reached.

- Don't tell lies.

For generations couples have been spending household finances on personal pleasure and lied to their partners about the cost. This is a recipe for disaster. Hiding new purchases about the house and spending more in the pub than one is prepared to admit are equally deceitful. We all have our foibles, but when only one of you is contributing to the household budget the other must observe respect in the expenditure of those finances.

A truly loving couple will read the bank statement together and this is a better indication of successful marriage than staring into each other's eyes over a bottle of wine. If you have overspent, be honest. Accept blame for the overdraft if it is genuinely your fault.

• Some budget better than others.

Allow the person with the astute mind to carry the cheque book and credit cards and not necessarily the person who earns more. Good marriage is as much about budgeting for success as anything else. Some of us are incapable of calculating even the simplest of household accounts and this has nothing to do with intellect. Practicality is a gift. Whosoever in the relationship has the most finely tuned practical skills should deal with the finances.

• Separate/joint accounts.

Whether or not you have joint or separate bank accounts is entirely dependent on your own attitude to money as an individual. If you have worked hard, when single, to earn and save money, you may not want immediately to put all your hard-earned cash into the bank account of someone else, no matter how much you may love them. On the other hand, if you both trust each other with money, then having a joint account will not bother you. Everyone has their own idea of what is best for them, and you ought to discuss this between you at length before reaching any major decisions. If necessary seek independent financial advice before handing over every penny, particularly if property is involved.

• Poverty.

It used to be said that 'when poverty comes in the door, love goes out the window'. Unfortunately, people who once expected never to be in the poverty trap are now finding themselves in that very position. But not every marriage that experiences severe financial hardship automatically breaks down. The terrible pressure that lack of money brings can permeate into your relationship and destroy it, but this does not have to be the case, if you try and work together as a unit.

Utilize the emotional as well as the financial resources of each other. Endeavour to support and comfort each other as best you can and bear in mind that although escaping from the relationship may seem the best way to alleviate financial pressure, it may make it worse. Do what you believe to be the best for yourself and those you love.

CAREERS

The relative job security enjoyed by previous generations does not and probably never will apply in the future. Even those careers which were considered foolproof guards against unemployment and financial insecurity are no longer as safe as they once were.

Couples about to marry need to prepare themselves for all sorts of re-adjustments in considering their future careers. As more and more people face unemployment and redundancy, we need to be prepared to compromise and remain open-minded in balancing our financial affairs.

There is no room for pride and self-seeking if you want to join together in a conciliatory way. A lot of families are now finding themselves being entirely supported by the income of the female and men are having to adjust to taking a fuller role in home and child care.

There are enormous social changes occurring in this generation and not since the last war has the role of women in the financial upkeep of the family been so vital.

Women are better educated and trained than in previous generations and evening classes are full of married women increasing and developing their skills. Traditional family roles are slowly disappearing and we are all facing periods of re-adjustment, not just in our attitudes to our partners but in our feelings about ourselves.

Too many people judge their value and self-worth by their career alone, so unemployment and redundancy are causing many marriage breakdowns as people, especially men, lose their self-esteem along with their jobs.

In order to alleviate this problem, couples need to look at their contribution to the upkeep of the family, not just in terms of financial input, but in emotional support, practical housecare, and judicious budgeting. Everything must be a team effort, with couples being prepared readily to adjust themselves to changes in the financial set up of the family, if and when they occur.

Role Switching

More and more women are working outside the home and are making new advances in professional status every day. It is a slow process but soon all traditionally held male professions are going to have their equal share of women and men are going to have to adopt new attitudes to cope with this.

This is not a bad thing. Many men have felt resentful in the past that the total responsibility for supporting the family has been down to them and an increasing number of men are realizing that they enjoy the daily work involved in raising a family. The important thing is to be prepared for readjustment and do not let pride stop you from taking on a new role. As much as possible ignore what you believe to be the pressures of society, build your family around your own ideals and be prepared to compromise. Nothing is forever and life is too short to miss out on trying something new because of misplaced pride.

Support each other in whatever you choose to do. Women are as entitled to their ambitions as men and men are entitled to admit they would prefer to be at home taking care of children. Many men who have lost their wives through illness and divorce and have been forced to take care of their children have found it a difficult but rewarding experience – and they are just as capable as women, when they have to be.

We all have differing skills and talents. The patience and energy required in raising children may easily be the forte of the husband. Continue to discuss these things between you and do not be ashamed of your choices. Remember, it is a free country and what works for others may not necessarily work for you.

Challenge conventional theories and try to look at life through the eyes of your partner. Endeavour to have an understanding of each other's needs within the framework of the relationship.

It has been predicted that in the future more and more people will choose to work from home. Part-time work and job sharing will become commonplace and even higher education and training may be carried out at home by use of video and computer technology. These are some of the new challenges which may face the generation of tomorrow and they alter all the usual perceptions of being employed and 'going out to work'. Yet again, it is up to each individual couple how they choose to adapt to these and other new choices facing them.

Success
Most people spend a great deal of time dreaming and planning for success. We work hard to study, train and build up our skills, in order to secure our futures. We all have an idea of what standard of living we think we need and in different ways we aim for that, along with professional recognition.

But when success actually comes, it can be extremely hard to cope with, especially if we are more successful that we set out to be. The run up to achievements can leave a feeling of emptiness after the event and some people will drive themselves to the limit longer than is necessary or healthy.

There are different ways in which achievements can be considered. Some people are driven to acquire more, long after success has been established and others are happy to settle with a modicum of success in one particular field and leave it at that.

Ambition
At different times in our lives we all have to work hard to achieve a cherished goal and most loving partners will endeavour to support each other at these times. However, it is not easy to live with someone who is ruthlessly ambitious for material and professional success, especially if it appears to be their *only* driving force. These people do not always have the patience and fortitude that make good marriages last. A person who continuously brings work home in the evenings

and weekends should not be surprised when their partner gets thoroughly fed up with it, especially when it impinges upon their lives over and above what is actually required.

Some people are capable of burying themselves in work, in order to avoid taking an honest look at themselves and their lives. There is no greater excuse for an emotionally reticent person than to be 'too busy' to talk to you. Workaholics are generally people whose lives are built on fear. They are usually very insecure and will work constantly rather than be 'found out'. Male workaholics make extremely bad husbands and any woman thinking that love will change a man like this is wrong. It is wise to be suspicious of anyone who claims to have to work 14 or more hours a day and the same at weekends and refuses to take holidays. No employer demands that much input, and you may find that the person who claims to be needed that much has a hidden emotional agenda that is best left to trained people to sort out. Workaholics always have relationship problems.

Expectations

We should be careful not to depend on our partner being successful in *everything* he/she does. There are worrying trends among some young women to aim to get a 'rich' husband, perhaps believing that to 'get' one is a form of success in itself. But money can be lost as well as won. Ill health and bad fortune can occur at any time, to any person, and a marriage based on material comfort will soon flounder when that comfort wanes.

Success can be anything we desire it to be. For some, it can be climbing a mountain or some other such personal ambition. For others it can be getting the promotion at work they have been aiming for. Success is relative to the individual, and like so many other aspects of our lives, can be controlled by the expectations of society rather than our own. We should be aiming for happiness and peace of mind and these are not always brought about by material possessions.

Aims and Desires

Sometimes we set our sights higher than we are capable of reaching, and although there is nothing wrong with aiming for the best that we can achieve, being driven by a desire for professional and material success can prevent us from appreciating other aspects of our lives.

For a young couple living in sub-standard accommodation, success can mean finding a home of their own and for a child with learning difficulties, success can mean acquiring the ability to read and write properly. In different communities success is measured by the economic and social dictates of that community.

Ideally what we should aim for is the fulfilment and happiness of ourselves *and* our families. Sometimes it is only when we re-direct our ambition and put other people first that we really start to achieve.

Any person with a powerful personal ambition which supersedes everything else is going to have to try and impart that passion to their partner. Men especially can feel very threatened by ambition in their wives, but it is not always the case. Besides, many men are reaching a stage whereby they have no choice but to defer to the skills of the women in their lives, whether as partners, friends, colleagues or employers, as women become more powerful in our community.

Setbacks

Our self-worth is dependent upon how we see our own potential and abilities. Throughout our lives we all suffer loss and setbacks and can sometimes feel valueless because we are not as successful as we had planned to be or as other people expected us to be. When we experience these inevitable setbacks it is important to feel that we have the support of our partner.

It is easier to cope with setbacks in life, if one is safe in the knowledge that professional failure will not necessarily destroy the marriage. When work difficulties arise, we should not let pride prevent us from leaning on those who we know will support us and be there for the bad times as well as the good. Setbacks can help us to re-evaluate ourselves and even turn us in a different and better direction. Married couples who have successfully dealt with professional and financial problems together and weathered the storm have a good understanding of these principles and a better chance of enjoying manifold years together.

Criticism and Support

The higher up the career ladder one goes, the more likely one is to be criticised. Coping with criticism takes strength and fortitude and it is important to realize this when balancing a career and married life.

If you are about to marry someone who has a career which involves high levels of stress, then be aware that you must be tolerant of their needs at home. Professional criticism can be borne if one has a supportive and loving family and as more women become, say, bank managers, lawyers, doctors and pilots themselves, they are going to need the type of support which they have been previously conditioned to give rather than receive.

One hurtful word from a partner can cause more damage than a torrent of professional rancour. When your partner walks through the door at the end of a day which has involved incredible stress, the last thing they want to hear from you is criticism. This is applicable to men and women. Please read the guidelines given in this book on how to communicate your point of view at a time and place when it will be listened to and absorbed and remember that even when you are married, kindness and good manners are simple to employ and far more effective than abuse.

SUMMARY

- No relationship can survive under the omnipresent threat of financial insecurity; this has little to do with the amount of revenue created but depends upon the couple's personal perception of the kind of lifestyle they want.
- Being 'rich' or 'poor' is relative, but you must agree on your perception of these two extremes. Look at the extremes of either poverty or wealth that would be likely to cause you problems.
- Fortunes can alter and change. 'Safe' career options no longer are.
- You are likely to argue more about money than anything else. It is the biggest single cause of marital breakdown.
- Learn to respect money and be aware of its power in your relationship with your partner.
- Prioritize. If you have an expensive hobby which your partner cannot share, be prepared for their disapproval if it impinges upon your household budget.
- Be honest about your expenditure and needs and discuss circumstances that may cause these to alter.

- Practicality is a gift. The most practical partner should take care of the finances, not necessarily the highest earner.
- Success should not always be measured by material gain.
- Emotional support is vital during times of difficulty at work.
- Respect and encourage each other's ambitions and goals.
- Be aware that setbacks are part of life. Be judicious in your criticism of other people's hopes and dreams.

FIVE

Sex

Sexual problems are the second major cause of marital breakdown. Despite the enormous amount of literature and media time devoted to the subject, many couples never reach the stage of sexual fulfilment which is possible for everyone.

If a good sex life is to be had, it helps to be in love. Not all couples who marry truly love each other and although they may have thrilling sex in the beginning of their relationship it is not enough to sustain a lifetime of commitment and will eventually become boring.

Making love can be one of the most life-enhancing experiences we will have and it is very different from having sex. However, even those couples who really do love one another can still experience sexual problems and these can permeate into every other part of our relationship.

Every one of us is concernèd about our sexuality at some stage in our lives. Few people go through adolescence and early adulthood without experiencing sexual fear and self-doubt. Unfortunately there remain a lot of misconceptions regarding sexual activity and inadequate advice for those about to embark on what they hope will be a lifetime union with one sexual partner.

In this chapter I will separate some advice for men and women as it appears that having sex with someone is much easier than talking about sex with someone. Women will talk to other women while men rarely feel capable of talking to anyone about their sexual fears and therein many problems lie.

THE FOLLOWING SECTION IS INTENDED FOR WOMEN

Growing Up

Our development as fully fledged sexual adults can be influenced by our conditioning as growing children. Parents tend to treat their male and female offspring differently with regard to their sexual growth. It is very difficult for a young girl from a sexually repressed family, for example, to discard that repression in adulthood. We are taught what nice girls do not do and although we are generally given information at school and home about the development of our bodies, little is still taught about the desires and needs of adult women.

It is wrong to suppose that women are less interested in sex and sexual matters than men. However, women tend to take longer fully to accept their normal desires and acquire the confidence to pursue them.

Learning about periods and babies is one thing. But young women are still not encouraged to appreciate themselves as sexual beings in the same way that men are. For that reason most women have very secret thoughts and aspirations which may be shared with trusted female friends but rarely with their male partners.

There remain some dreadful double standards in society's reaction to female sexuality. Young men who wish to 'sow their wild oats' are almost encouraged and rarely derided for that behaviour. Young women who even dare to express such desires are classed as 'tarts' or 'slags'. No-one would want to be branded with such a title. These words or similar phrases are incredibly offensive and no such male equivalent exists.

So women tend to keep their thoughts and fantasies to themselves – it is hardly surprising. How ever many sexual partners a women may have she still may not feel able to be a truly free sexual human being with her husband and the fear of derision can force some women into being sexually repressed throughout their married lives.

Freedom

The key to good sex is freedom of expression. We have control over how many children we have. We know how to protect ourselves against disease. We may have fallen in love with someone and are planning to marry and yet so many of us are still incapable of fully expressing our sexual desires.

It takes an enormous amount of courage to be totally trusting of anyone, especially men. Older women or those in a second marriage or long-term relationship may have gained the experience and knowledge to enjoy their sexual activity fully but for younger women in a first major relationship it can be very difficult indeed.

Self-Love

The most potent sexual organ in the body of a woman is her brain.

Recent surveys have shown that young women masturbate as frequently as men. Masturbation requires fantasy and as women are not encouraged to voice their desires they became adept at keeping their sexual thoughts to themselves. Every person who has ever masturbated will know what a pleasant and relieving experience it can be and in order fully to appreciate sex with anyone else it helps to have as much knowledge as possible as to how your own body works, and how and where you liked to be touched and stimulated.

Learning to love and appreciate your own needs will help you to impart that information to your partner. In some societies female masturbation is still considered shameful and most women would be embarrassed and frightened to admit that they even think about it. But it is obvious that most women at least try it and many thoroughly enjoy it, whether in a relationship or not.

Talking

However, it need not be the secret garden which we pretend it is. If you have never discussed this subject before, try talking to trusted female friend about it. You may be surprised what an interesting and informative discussion it can be. Women are quite capable of talking to each other about PMT and coils but there are other more interesting subjects for feminine debate and it helps to remove the guilt that is normally associated with female self-love.

Information on this subject is not generally found and although men may think they have 'cornered the market' on self-love, they are wrong. We all have our thoughts and desires and we are equally entitled to them. Do not wait until you are sexually dissatisfied before you learn openly to discuss sexual matters, including the pursuit of pleasure and masturbation. It is, after all, the safest sex you can have. All the humorous quips attached to masturbation relate to men 'doing it', while women smile coyly and pretend not to understand. Is it any wonder we have so much trouble admitting to our desires, even to the person we love most of all.

Guilt

This has got to be one of the biggest passion killers known

to womankind and it can lead of a whole set of totally unnecessary anxieties.

Guilt and good sex do not make happy bedfellows. But many young females still experience enormous feelings of shame that seem to coincide with passion. Along with healthy lust come fear and guilt and many women are stuck between both, not quite knowing what to do.

It is very hard for some women to face up to their desires and eliminate sexual guilt from their lives. Our social programming informs us that we should not get the same lusts as men, but we do. We stay quiet about it, but we still feel the same.

Sex aids, toys and manuals are being bought by women in large numbers, but they tend to be purchased by older women who have reached a stage in their lives where they have realized that it's quite okay to enjoy good, honest, lusty sex and to admit to it. But younger women appear not to have that confidence and that is why so many young couples, riddled with guilt and self-doubt have sexual problems which are bad enough to destroy their marriages.

It's not easy suddenly to rid yourself of this, but if you are about to get married and you are experiencing feelings of sexual guilt, there are psychosexual counsellors who can help you. It is important to accept that your feelings are normal and felt by everyone at some stage or other. But guilt can really cripple your self-assurance and prevent you from projecting yourself in a sexual way, despite what passion may linger beneath.

A good lover is proud of her desires and is keen to develop and explore them further. Every single one of us has sexual urges – it is what keeps the world peopled. How we respond to those urges is entirely up to the individual, but it helps not to feel guilty about something which is a normal part of humanity. When you have genuinely done something that deserves guilt then guilt can help you realize that what you have done has injured someone else and should prevent you from doing it again. Guilt needs to be put into perspective and it has no place in the bedroom.

Female Bisexuality

One of the most common sexual fantasies for women involves making love with another woman. This is pretty normal and does not make you a lesbian. For women who feel even mildly threatened by intercourse with a man, the thought of being in a less vulnerable position can be very enticing. One would argue that there is beauty in both male and female bodies and our minds are free to imagine what they like.

However, some women find that they are capable of not just fantasizing about being with other women, but that they also have strong emotional feelings for individual women and are capable of truly loving both sexes.

If you think you may feel like this and are about to enter a marriage, then it would be wise to talk to a bisexual counsellor first. Do not rush to talk to your partner about it, because he may not wish to understand. It does not mean that you cannot have a successful and loving marriage, but you must try to determine, before getting married, if you will be capable of putting that aspect of your sexuality aside. A lot of people have bi-sexual desires and never admit to them; if you feel that you will be able to maintain this silence then carry on. However, it may be better to continue self-exploration before settling down into a marriage, because sexual awareness plays an enormous part in the success of any relationship.

Relating to Him

Now that you have come to terms with a few facts, it's time

to impart that information to your partner. First try and ensure a few things apply. Do you love him? Sex is *always* better with someone you love, if you get the sex right. Despite what techniques and manuals another man may use, there is no better feeling than making love, with the man you love. It is a total physical and emotional union and couples who love each other and have good sex, make love frequently and stay faithful for years. Love like this is available to all.

Once you have established an emotional bond and are prepared to trust each other completely and where possible make a commitment to each other, then it's time to consider your sexual relationship. But first of all you must examine your own attitude, as an individual. Women who have never practised self-love before should try it. If you know how to turn yourself on, it will be easier for you to show him, and it helps to keep you in touch with your own desires and the workings of your body. There are books and videos available to help you, if you feel you need them; if you are embarrassed about requesting these, then get them by mail order.

Talk Again

Do not expect your partner instinctively to know how to please you. No matter how much experience he may have had with other women, we are all different and our bodies react in different ways to stimulation. If you have a good understanding of your own body and what pleases you, then you are in a good position to show him as well. Do not keep sexual discussion for the bedroom. Get accustomed to talking about your sexuality with him while you are not in bed together. Ask him what he likes and what in the past has turned him on. Do not be worried about any previous sexual experience he may or may not have had, he is with you now and you are the one that matters.

We bring with us into the bedroom all the experience of our lives and it is wrong to try to dismiss the past entirely. Used constructively, past experience can enhance our present relationships.

Show Him
Without droning on about your own sexual history, gently inform him of anything which you feel you would like and things you are sure that you would dislike. Kiss and touch the parts of his body upon which you also like to be kissed and touched. Take his hands and gently guide them to where you want them to be. Voice your approval when he does something you particularly like and don't be ashamed to show him the most intimate places on your body. Give him plenty of verbal encouragement and try to look relaxed. If there is a particular position that you have always wanted to try, then guide him to you in that way. Do not always expect him to take the lead. At different times in our lives, such as during pregnancy, we will have to try new positions, but you do not have to wait until then. You will find that there are certain positions which make it easier for you to achieve an orgasm, and the missionary position is not the best. So take the lead and try new things, buy a manual and read it carefully, then show your man what you like. He will love it.

What He Wants
Ask your partner - outside the bedroom - what he really wants in bed. Ask him at a moment when you can expect an honest answer and do try to keep an open mind about his response. Men usually enjoy sexual adventure and variation but they can have some pretty weird fantasies, just like you, and it can help you enormously to find out what

they are. It is surprising how ashamed men can be of their own eroticism. He may be into pornography and want to share that with you but is frightened to ask. He may even want to dress up in a particular way or want you to, but whatever it is, it is important that you, as his wife, are aware of his desires and dreams. Some men also enjoy having with sex with a woman who is partially clothed and not completely naked. To find out what your husband likes, just ask him and if he doesn't mention any of the above, then you raise the subject.

Most men have fantasies about sleeping with two women at the same time, but few ever get the chance to try. If he suggests it, it would be wise for you to refuse. Introducing anyone else into your love life is a dangerous game to play and should be avoided at all costs.

Oral Sex

In countries where female virginity is held in high esteem, young women become accustomed to performing oral sex on their boyfriends and fiancés long before vaginal intercourse is experienced. For them it appears to be the most natural way to satisfy their partners while maintaining an intact hymen and avoiding pregnancy. However, in the West, women tend to think of sex in terms of intercourse first and variations on it second. Oral sex is usually high on any man's sexual agenda, and there are large numbers of men who go to prostitutes for this particular service alone.

It is entirely up to the individual woman whether or not she chooses to indulge in oral sex. However, it must be remembered that images thereof take up pages and pages of male pornography and for most men it is a common fantasy and desire. In fact some men admit to preferring it to intercourse. Whatever you decide between you on this issue is okay, but it is wise to discuss it. Oral sex (for both of you) can be a wonderful lesson in intimate loving and involves placing an enormous amount of trust in each other, but as with every other aspect of sexuality, it is only alright when you are both comfortable with it. Try it and see.

Hang Ups

Many women, given the chance to look at their naked body in a mirror, will immediately spot something they do not like. There are enormous pressures put on women to fit into what society has deemed is beautiful. In its most extreme form this can lead to anorexia and bulimia and even to dangerous and unnecessary cosmetic surgery. The vast majority of people who are actively trying to alter their shape, whether through diet, exercise or surgery, are women.

We appear to take this for granted. But in reality it is a frightening indictment of our present culture. Men simply do not have the same pressure to conform to beauty stereotypes.

If you are constantly worried about the design of your body then it is impossible to have really great sex. We are all different and unless your health is being affected by some aspect of your body shape, then try not to worry about it too much, especially in bed.

It will be difficult for you to try various sexual positions if you are paranoid about the shape of your thighs or the size of your bottom. Just because you think you are not attractive does not mean that you are right. A relaxed lover is a good lover, and the happiest people are those who have come to accept themselves for what they are. Remember, if a man is lying in bed with you and obviously wants to make love to you, then no matter what you think of yourself, he must be quite happy or he would not be there. No one will ever judge a woman more harshly than she judges herself.

So forget your cellulite for a couple of hours and get on

with it. You are an individual and your attitude to yourself is what makes you truly sexy. Even the most beautiful women in the world have parts of themselves which they despise. Your relaxed and carefree state of mind is what will really turn him on.

FOR BOTH OF YOU

Resentments
Never give in to a sexual request that you are really unhappy about, especially if it involves other people. Sexual resentments can destroy your relationship and if you feel that your partner is making any sort of demand which is causing you to suffer then put a stop to it. Each couple must find their own boundaries, but men frequently complain that there are certain things that they really want which they cannot get at home. If this becomes a real problem, then you should both try some form of sexual counselling.

Do not be afraid to learn as much as you can about sex and sexual matters. We are all entitled to a rich and fulfilling sex life and making love is one of the best ways of relieving stress and tension. It can also enhance your relationship and bring you closer together. But being forced into performing any kind of sexual act which you find abhorrent is abuse. You cannot expect your relationship to work if you are resentful of each other's demands or rejections. You must talk resentments through, especially sexual resentments.

Other People
Do not be concerned about what you think other people are doing. Many people exaggerate their sexual expertise and history and few will admit when they are having problems,

even though *all* of us experience some form of sexual difficulty in our lives.

Do not believe that everyone else is having a wild time and you are not. Your sex life is between you and your partner and what you do and how often you do it is up to you both. Friends and colleagues may make their own sex lives sound fantastic and you are bound to compare yourself unfavourably with them. But all that matters is that you are happy with your own set up. There remains a lot of shame and dishonesty in regard to sexual matters, so ignore people who boast about it, they are probably deeply insecure; it's better to follow your own instincts.

Communication
Good communication is vital to good sex and talking to each other about your most intimate desires can be a marvellous turn on. Some men turn to affairs and even prostitutes to have a particular sexual experience which they are too embarrassed to ask their wives for. As far as bedroom etiquette is concerned, anything goes, as long as you are both comfortable with it. Do not be frightened to ask. Finding out what you both really like is an enormously freeing experience. There is no joy in ignorance, nor in pretending that things are well when they are not. Both men and women are capable of incredible dishonesty in bed and it does not make for fulfilling sex. Don't lie to each other, 'fake it', or pretend to be coy. Be honest and your partner should follow suit.

Intercourse and Other Things
Sex does not always have to be about intercourse. There are many other ways of enjoying regular sexual activity without expecting full intercourse every time. Any form of intimate

touching and kissing could be considered a sexual experience and when one or both partners have a busy job, then it helps to find ways in which you can satisfy each other without expending all your energy.

Some evenings we like to go out and have a three-course meal and spend time eating and drinking in a leisurely and relaxed manner. At other times all we need is a quick sandwich. Good sex is a bit like that. It should fit in with your lifestyle. Besides, if a man thinks that every time he wants an orgasm it will involve hours of foreplay then he is less likely to suggest it and more likely to masturbate in the bathroom without his partner, as is the woman who is too tired to have intercourse but would still like some form of satisfaction. Sexually experienced women are aware of these factors and can therefore help to dispel myths regarding their own differing and changing needs.

So try and find ways of enjoying regular sex that does not always require you both to spend a long time in the preparation. A 'quickie' can be just as much fun as any other form of intercourse, as can mutual masturbation and oral sex. This does not mean that you should dispense with foreplay and turn your sex life into a series of fast and furious events. Just open your mind to the choices. Times, places, situations and emotions all have a part to play in how we relate to each other sexually. The most important thing is to be aware of the possibilities.

Fidelity

When most people first get married they expect and indeed promise to be faithful to one another for the rest of their lives. In the early flush of love that can seem like an easy promise to make and one that is usually taken with total sincerity. However, fidelity can be difficult to maintain, especially a few years into the marriage when pressures over careers, money and children can make the relationship appear difficult in itself and other 'encounters' seem incredibly appealing.

There are many and varied reasons why people start to look outside the relationship for some form of sexual or emotional satisfaction. Some find it difficult to derive all their stimulation from one other individual and others genuinely believe they have 'fallen in love' with someone other than the person they initially chose to love, honour and cherish.

But whatever the criteria, infidelity always causes pain and guilt and frequently has disastrous consequences for the marriage. Women are almost as likely as men to be unfaithful but usually for quite different reasons. However, it helps to establish in your mind as much as you can before you marry, that the person you have chosen will provide as much sexual love and emotional support as you will need. Self-awareness is therefore vital if acrimonious scenes are to be avoided later on.

Few people decide to be unfaithful and it generally happens by accident, but the damage that can ensue is enormous and no one should allow themselves to be drawn into this situation without a great deal of thought and personal evaluation.

If you feel that your relationship has deteriorated to the extent that you are considering taking a lover then you must talk to your partner about your feelings and what you can both do to rectify the situation. Infidelity is not just about sex and lust - frequently people are looking for love and approval as well and even a shoulder to cry on or friendship. But whatever it is you are seeking elsewhere, you must try to find out what has gone wrong in your relationship for you to be thinking of involving another person in your life.

Ask yourself if the affair would be worth the pain and anguish your partner would inevitably suffer and the feelings of the third party must also be considered. No-one is free to be a moral judge of another and we are all capable of seeing beauty in others and of being attracted to various people. But if this is seriously threatening your marriage, then counselling should be sought, to get to the basis of the problem, before you embark on an affair that could end up ruining your life and that of your partner.

There is a difference between a drunken liaison and a full-scale love affair but whatever the situation, the consequences remain dire. Couples who have a fulfilling sexual relationship and make love frequently are less likely to want or need an extra-marital affair as are those who are capable of sharing all their emotional needs and have a good level of communication. Even people with strong moral and religious beliefs are still capable of affairs and none of us are immune from the possibility. But it is not an inevitable occurrence and many thousands of people have long and happy marriages without ever indulging in an extra-marital affair. As with every other aspect of our relationship, love is not enough, but trust, honesty, freedom and respect will enable us to make the right decision if infidelity seems likely.

Do not be afraid to seek guidance if you are caught in an emotional dilemma like this. There are plenty of services available to help us cope with problems of this nature. Remember it may not be an affair that you are seeking, but some other form of comfort, approval or recognition. If your sexual relationship with your partner is unsatisfactory, you cannot be sure that someone else would be better. You just do not know and unfaithfulness can be dangerous in our present climate, so think very carefully before acting on an impulse that involves deceit, lies and even physical danger.

THIS SECTION IS INTENDED FOR MEN

Despite the number of surveys and amount of research given to understanding male sexuality, there is actually very little known about it, as most people do not read surveys and men are notoriously bad at talking about their sexual feelings. There can be a lot of bravado and boasting when men get together, but most of this is sexist nonsense and few men are really prepared to discuss, either among themselves or with their partners, how they really feel.

The most common complaint women have about their partners is that 'he won't talk to me'. This is hardly surprising given that men are discouraged from expressing emotion almost from the day they learn to speak. This puts an awful amount of pressure on men to be strong and silent at times when women are 'allowed' to express themselves fully and emotional reticence is a common cause of sexual dysfunction.

Women expect men automatically to 'know' what to do, especially in bed. Unfortunately, men as well as women have to learn how to be good and open lovers, free of guilt and honest enough to vent their true desires. Talking to other men is unlikely to help as men do not appear to tell each other if they are having any type of sexual problem.

Pornography

Most men at different stages in their lives, but particularly when young, are interested in pornography, especially when sexual exploration is at its height. Pictures of naked, appealing and apparently 'ready' women are exciting for most and pornographic stories help in masturbation. But where pornography fails men is in helping them to understand the women in their lives and especially wives and girlfriends.

Women in pornography are fictional, they do not exist. They are the product of the imagination of someone else and the stories and pictures are well designed to provide titillation and desire, but nothing else. Do not expect ordinary women to behave in the way that pornographic images dictate.

If you want to continue enjoying pornography after marriage, do not expect your partner necessarily to understand your need. Some women do find these images as much a turn on as men, but most feel very threatened by it and see it as a form of disloyalty on the part of their husbands. Talk about it together, but be prepared for her disapproval: it takes an extremely open-minded and adventurous woman to accept this.

Fantasy

It is commonly thought that men think about sex several times every hour and are liable to be turned on by almost any woman at any time. What this theory does not tell us is that men are individuals and like women they have their own private images of what constitutes desirability and what does not. Common male fantasies are threesomes, voyeurism, quick sex with strangers, bondage, dressing up and homosexuality. When married, a man commits himself to one sexual partner for the rest of his life. To what level he intends to indulge his fantasies is partly dependent on what his partner is happy to comply with, but he may also hold certain fantasies that he has no intention of ever trying to fulfil.

For men, as with women, it is important to establish before marriage what each partner considers are the safe boundaries in the quest for sexual fulfilment. Every couple is different, and happy couples are those who have discovered true satisfaction with each other using whatever method suits them both.

If a man feels that there is something about which he cannot talk to his wife, but which he still has an urge to fulfil, then he needs to speak to someone about it, especially if it involves any kind of homosexual experience.

Male Bisexuality

Even the most heterosexual man alive has at some time thought about a homosexual encounter. Most men would vehemently deny this, but an honest man will tell you that it has at some stage, particularly as an adolescent, 'crossed his mind'. As with women, this does not mean that the man is therefore 'gay', but to some men the very nature of a homosexual experience can seem appealing. Sex with another man can appear enticing in that it involves no risk of pregnancy and can be perceived as a more 'casual' encounter than that with a woman. Of course, not all homosexual experiences are 'casual' experiences but to a heterosexual man, it can seem less complicated and emotionally draining than straight sex.

It is much easier for a man to have a homosexual encounter than it is for a woman. Male 'gay' bars and clubs are more plentiful than female equivalents and in most cities, these places are well known and easily frequented. Many 'out' homosexual men have had married lovers and most women would be shocked and hurt to discover their partner had experienced an encounter of this kind.

If, as a married man, or a man considering marriage, you are having strong desires for homosexual experiences and you honestly believe it may affect in some way your relationship with your wife, then you must contact an organization that can provide sexual counselling for you. Heterosexual men are capable of 'gay' fantasy but when this borders over into real desire, it can become difficult to maintain a heterosexual relationship.

Physical Dysfunction

The most common sexual dysfunctions in men are premature ejaculation and impotence. Most men experience these to a greater or lesser degree at some stage in their sexual lives and they are usually easily treated.

Premature ejaculation can be caused by performance anxiety and fear of not pleasing your partner. There are mental and physical techniques which can be taught to treat this problem successfully and an understanding partner always helps. Do not let performance pressure prevent you from enjoying good sex. Women can be sexually stimulated in a variety of ways and penetrative sex is not the only way to arouse and satisfy your partner. If this is becoming a problem for you, talk to your General Practitioner first to establish that there is no physical cause, then get hold of any good manual covering this subject and practice with your partner. Do not let it spoil your sex life, as, with patience and trust, it can generally be overcome.

Most men go through a period of impotence at some time and although distressing, it usually rectifies itself after a while. Common causes are overwork, stress and general tiredness. If impotence is lasting longer than a few days, your doctor is the best person to advise you how to deal with it. The important rule is not to be alarmed by sudden impotence - it does happen to practically everyone.

SUMMARY FOR BOTH OF YOU

- Love.
    Sex is always better with someone you love. If you truly love each other but are experiencing sexual difficulties, seek counselling and get hold

of as much advice and information as you can. Do not allow sexual problems to ruin your relationship, as most are easily treated with patience, trust and an open-minded willingness to try.

- Discussion.

  Try to talk to each other about sex and sexual matters. Honest communication is vital if you are going to get to know each other fully. Correct information is always better than guesswork and talking about sex can be very erotic.

- Honesty.

  Endeavour to express yourself honestly with your partner. There is no point in pretending that you like something just because you do not want to hurt the other's feelings. They would be more hurt if they knew you were lying.

- Guilt.

  Do not feel guilty about having strong sexual desires and needs. Without them the human race would not exist. They are a gift to be enjoyed, so don't be ashamed of something which has been bestowed upon every one of us.

- Self-Image.

  Do not let a bad self-image prevent you from enjoying a healthy sex life. If you are frightened to project yourself in a sexual way because of your self-image, then seek counselling to alter this. Remember that to be constantly bringing yourself down is an insult to your partner. They have seen something in you to love and you have no right to denigrate their opinion.

- Self-Exploration.

  It is easier to impart your needs to your partner if you are fully aware of what they are. Get into the habit of touching and appreciating your own body and its response to different forms of stimuli. Our needs are constantly changing, so let self-exploration became a natural, normal routine.

- Ignore other people's sex lives.

  Bearing in mind that few people are totally honest when discussing sex in an open environment such as a pub or canteen, they cannot always be trusted. Therefore do not compare your own sex life unfavourably with that of *anyone* else. Work on what goes well for you and your partner.

- Don't let set-backs put you off.

  We all experience set-backs at different times in our lives. Do not be put off just because it may not go right initially. Good sex takes a bit of time to engender and discovery is part of the fun.

- Touching.

  Get into the habit of touching and kissing each other outside the bedroom. Affection costs nothing and can ease a whole manner of ills. Learn a little about basic massage techniques and practice on one another. It will make sex more interesting and generate relaxation and comfort, apart from bringing you closer together.

- Intercourse.

  Sex does not always have to be full intercourse. There are many different ways you can find to stimulate and satisfy each other apart from penetration. Explore these possibilities, as you will not always have the energy and strength required to indulge in long sexual rituals, and it does not mean that you cannot please each other in some way.

- AIDS/HIV

Unfortunately, it is now impossible to address any issues surrounding sexuality without commenting on AIDS and HIV. There remains a considerable amount of fear and ignorance regarding this infection, but most of us should at least be aware that the best way to guard against becoming infected is to endeavour to remain within monogamous relationships and practise safe sex, particularly the use of condoms, at all times.

However, as this book is aimed at those planning to marry and possibly have children, then at some stage safe sex may be abandoned in order for conception to take place.

If you feel that you may have been, at some stage in your life, at risk from contracting the HIV virus, talk to an AIDS counsellor, who can be contacted through the National Aids Helpline, The Terrence Higgins Trust, or the STD Clinic of your local hospital. Your fears may very well be unfounded, but it is much better to enter a new relationship in the full knowledge that you are not likely inadvertently to cause harm to someone you love.

SIX

Children

Most people expect at some time in their lives to have children. They can arrive by accident, of course – even in these days of free and available contraception for all, a lot of unplanned pregnancies still occur, especially in the very young. And when a young couple fall in love and get married, it does not take long before friends and relatives are inquiring as to when they are going to 'start a family'; it is expected that this is something they will want to do.

Many people feel that to live their lives without having experienced parenthood leads to an empty and lonely existence; the pressure on us to procreate can be strong indeed.

An attack of broodiness can happen at any time and when couples are very much in love, having children seems like an obvious way of progressing on in their relationship.

Our society is geared around the family unit and people who choose not to have children are considered selfish and cold. This is unfortunate as the world is so grossly overpopulated and couples who decide not to bring more children into the world should not be subjected to criticism.

However, at the beginning of marriage, the issue regarding children has to be considered very seriously indeed. Having a child is the biggest responsibility we are ever likely to take on. Marriage, job and mortgage may seem enormous in themselves, but they pale into insignificance when compared to the total responsibility of parenthood.

However, there are certain aspects of child-rearing that are rarely discussed and there are reasons why childless people are not always given the best advice.

Here are some facts to be considered before coming off the pill or throwing your condoms away.

- A baby is not an extension of you and your loved one.

   It is a person with a personality and look all of its own. Couples dream of having a child that will be a symbol of their togetherness. The genetic makeup of a child comes from various different sources and it may not necessarily have your sweet temperament and your partner's blue eyes. It will be what it will be and you may not always like what you produce. Our children are on loan to us and may not always give back the enormous amount of investment we put into them, nor should we expect it.

- Children are small adults.

   They are not dolls to be dressed, played with and discarded. They are people, like you or I and will be as individual as everyone else in the world. Do not think that your baby will shine in any particular way, just because it is yours. You do not know what he or she will be like until their own character begins to emerge.

- They are expensive to keep.

   If you were asked to look after a dependent friend or relative but deduced that you could not afford it, then neither can you afford to have a child. They cost a fortune. Unless you have worked out all the financial obligations you are going to have in the following years, then don't even consider getting pregnant. Financial problems are the single biggest cause of marital breakdown. Babies are not cheap just because they are small and relatively easy to acquire. They are

the biggest financial drain known to man - and woman.
If you are prepared to do without things which you
have always taken for granted then fine, but remember,
once the child is born, it should be the greatest
priority in your life and you have to be ready for that.

- Are you *both* ready?

Have a look at your relationship. Do you think your
partner will be helpful and supportive, or unlikely to
take on a fair share of the child-rearing? If neither of
you lives close to your families, you are going to have
to rely on each other for support. Are both of you
prepared to do that? If neither of you has much
experience looking after children, then the whole thing
will come as a bit of a shock. Are you both going to
carry on working and if not who is going to take care
of the child? Talk about it.

- How is your relationship?

Do not believe that having a child will make a
difficult marriage better or suddenly induce you to love
each other in a new way. Your love and commitment
to each other must be as firmly grounded as is possible
before you consider introducing a new person into it.
Many people have had babies in the misconception that
it will improve a poor relationship. The strain of child-
rearing is more likely to exacerbate marriage difficulties
and staying together for the sake of children can lead
to wasteful years of resentment and frustration.

- Do either of you have any childhood resentments of
your own?

Think seriously about your own childhood. Ask
yourself if it was as happy as you would have liked. If
your parents held resentments in their own lives, is it
likely that they may have passed them on to you? Do
you feel free of childhood pains yourself? If not,

remember that bad cycles in families are not easy to break. Are your brothers and sisters happy and fulfilled people? Do not have a baby to fill an empty place in your own emotional life. If you feel that you need extra love and approval yourself do not expect a child to provide it. It will fulfil certain criteria, but it is not there to make you feel better about yourself.

- Ignore the procreation of others.

If you see siblings, cousins or friends having children, do not let that influence you in any way to have children of your own. However other people wish to live their lives has no bearing on how you live yours. If you want attention and approval from other members of your family, having a baby may seem like the best way of achieving it. But their approval or indeed disapproval is not a yardstick by which to measure your own value. People will always be having babies. It does not mean that you have to.

- Self-awareness.

Just as it is important to be as aware of your own needs and desires before getting married, it is even more important to have adequate self-awareness before having children. If you are bored with your job or feel undervalued within the framework of your family, having a baby will not suddenly give you the sense of value that you seek. There are other ways of seeking self-fulfilment, with less catastrophic results when things start to become difficult. You should never have a baby as an 'insurance policy' against career failure.

A child is with you for life. Even after it leaves home and develops a life of its own, having a child will alter your life forever. No parent can ever fully let go of the bonds they have with their children – even those who choose to have their babies adopted, never, ever forget them.

- You do not have to get pregnant to raise children.

There are homes all over the world packed with abandoned and unwanted children. There are couples who aim to adopt these children but usually because they are medically incapable of having children of their own. Adopting or fostering children is always regarded as second best to having your 'own baby' and I believe that we should change our attitude to this.

Parenting is a very emotive issue, but if you are determined to be a parent and find that you have the financial capability and the extra love and energy required, why not consider adopting or fostering other people's children even though you are capable of having children of your own.

If you are not expecting a small imitation of yourself then it is worth talking about. Childless couples frequently complain that there are not enough babies available for adoption. But this is primarily because they are seeking children as young as possible and as similar to them both as they can get. There is understandable logic in this and it is something which learned teams of social service officers have discovered to be for the best.

However, just because a child may be older than new-born, come from a different ethnic background to you, or have some form of disability, does not mean that you will not love him/her, nor that you will have less experience of the true joy of parenting.

It is a natural urge to want to reproduce yourself. But not everyone can and this means that some children who would normally end up in orphanages are adopted by people who genuinely love and care for them. There are plenty of children like that. Think about it.

- Do you agree about what is 'correct parenting'?

  Do not wait until the child is born to discuss the changes that it will make to your life. Are one or both of you going to take responsibility for discipline and training? Do you agree as to how much or how little family revenue should be devoted to the child's education? If you had quite a different upbringing from your partner, you may find problems when you have children of your own. For example, one of you may believe wholeheartedly in corporal punishment or private education and the other may be strongly opposed to it. The problem with having children is that we really do not know what the child will be like until it is born, but you *must* decide between you, as much as you can, how you intend to raise your children. You cannot use a child as a 'tennis ball' between each other, vying for power over that child and always assuming that your way is right. As I have said many times before in this book, talk about it!

- Are you absolutely sure you both want children?

  It's surprising how many people wait until after they are married before really addressing this issue. It is easy to put off such discussions until later, but it will crop up again. If you truly believe that parenting is not for you and that that is unlikely to change, then for the sake of your partner, tell them. Do not pretend that it is something you may be prepared to do later in life when you know that is not the case. Not all of us are happy with the prospect of having children and this is nothing to be ashamed of.

REASONS NOT TO HAVE CHILDREN

It is surprising how many people have children for the strangest reasons. Here are ten good reasons NOT to have children.

1. You are bored with your life and want a change of routine.
2. You want to feel important to other family members.
3. You feel of less value in society because you are childless.
4. Friends and relatives are having children.
5. You want to solidify a shaky relationship.
6. You are feeling unloved and are seeking approval.
7. You had a bad childhood yourself and want to recreate and 'improve' it through your own children.
8. You want to feel permanently linked to your partner.
9. You want to be entitled to some form of state benefit (even though it is never enough).
10. You no longer want to be responsible for yourself and you think by having a child that people and/or society will 'look after you'.

None of the above are sensible reasons for taking on the most demanding role we are ever likely to face. Happy and fulfilled couples are more likely to raise happy and fulfilled children. If you feel any of the emotions expressed above, seek ways of dealing with those feelings other than having a baby. Our children deserve the best we can give them and this is not about toys, bikes and videos. Children need warmth, understanding, patience, gentle guidance and above all else, parents who are not harbouring resentments of their own.

For Women

In most relationships the female takes responsibility for contraception. This is because most devices are developed to prevent pregnancy occurring in women. Throughout your life, your choice and method of contraception will change, but in your early and most fertile years, if you do not want to get pregnant, be stringent in your attitude. Many people have and continue to get pregnant by accident. In a time when adequate contraception is freely available the statistics for unwanted pregnancy remain as high as ever and in fact are increasing.

Most modern contraceptive devices, when used properly, are highly successful in preventing pregnancy, yet so many people claim that they got 'caught' or 'fell pregnant'. Could it be because people feel passionate when they least expect to and do not have a suitable device at hand? If so, the simple remedy is to carry condoms everywhere you go. If however, you are taking the Pill and still get 'caught' you must ask yourself how and why this happened. Did you really want to get pregnant but were frightened to admit to it?

If you were relying on either the withdrawal or the rhythm method, then it is not surprising that you became pregnant. The simple fact is that neither of these two methods are remotely reliable. Before withdrawal, some semen can escape even though ejaculation has not occurred and even if your partner argues that he will be 'careful', you would be unwise to rely on that. Even the most careful men become fathers without intending to.

If you are having sex during or around the time of your period in the belief that you are 'safe' from pregnancy, then you are wrong. Sperm can remain in the womb for several days and although the rhythm method may work for some people some of the time, it is simply not reliable enough to work for every couple every time.

It is very tempting for an insecure woman to feel that pregnancy is her only choice in life. Some women still attempt to trap men into marriage by getting pregnant. This is a dangerous and cruel trick to play on him, yourself and your child. If someone loves you and cares for you it is because of yourself. There is something about you as an individual which they will choose to love or not as the case may be. Do not believe that his feelings towards you will change, just because you are having his child. If he does not want children then he will resent you for having conned him. Do not even think about it.

For Men

It should not be forgotten that responsibility for planned parenthood is a joint venture. Although most contraceptive devices are made for women to use, some can have serious drawbacks. Not every woman can cope with the difficulties associated with the contraceptive pill, the coil, the 'cap' or the female condom.

At different times in your lives together you may alter your chosen method of contraception; for example, it is inadvisable for women to take the contraceptive pill for long periods of time, especially if they are smokers. You should therefore become accustomed to changing the method you use according to your changing needs.

The most reliable form of contraception a man can use is the condom. Some men are opposed to using this method for a variety of reasons, but condoms when used properly have an excellent success rate and pose the least risk to the health and well-being of the woman. Some men complain that this 'barrier' method reduces their enjoyment, but condoms can be obtained in all shapes and sizes and can become quite erotic sex aids. They can also delay ejaculation slightly in some men which can increase pleasure for both partners.

A truly responsible man will be prepared to open his mind to the different methods available, but your top priority should be the health, well-being and pleasure of you both.

SUMMARY

- Unless you are psychologically prepared for the emotional battlefield that is parenthood, then don't consider it.
- Make sure that you are prepared to give up the freedom which you may take for granted – including most of your leisure time.
- Be ready to look at life less selfishly than you ever have before.
- As much as possible ensure that your relationship can withstand the difficulties that always ensue with parenthood.
- Prepare yourselves physically for the hard work of pregnancy, childbirth and the early years. No job you have ever undertaken before demands as many hours and as much effort as child-rearing.
- Look at your bank account and be prepared for its depletion. Do not underestimate the cost of children.
- Not all children are born healthy, normal and balanced. Some have extra difficulties and problems.
- Forget all the clichés attached to parenting. Above all else it is a demanding, time-consuming, all-encompassing, job of work. Albeit with some

reward, but not always as much as you will expect.

- If you have little contact with children, try to have some. Baby sitting for friends and relatives is a good way of finding out a little of the commitment involved.
- Ask *yourself* honestly, if you really want to be a parent. There is no shame in being true to yourself and it will save terrible problems later on.
- If you do have a child, remember that your life will never be the same again.

SEVEN

Emotional and Physical Health

At the very beginning of a relationship, most couples, who are in the main young and in good health, expect that the way they think, feel and act today, will be the way they think, feel and act, forever.

There are some sad facts to be taken into consideration before getting married and committing yourself to one person for the rest of your life.

The main consideration is something that I have previously touched upon and that is personal change.

EMOTIONAL MATURITY

I have stressed the importance of gaining emotional maturity before getting married. As we grow and develop as individuals, so we expect our relationship to coincide with these changes.

Unfortunately, one third of Western marriages last on average nine years. The other two thirds may last for much longer or until one of the partners dies, but not all are happy unions and many people stay together due to fear of loneliness and social and financial change.

Successful marriages are those in which the couples have found a mutual understanding, respect and trust and they have fully accepted their partner for what they are and continue to love them for that. However, we all have our own personalities, foibles and psychological make-up. The more self-worth we achieved as single people the better chance our marriage has of succeeding.

Some of us are more likely to want the solidity of marriage than others and there are some people who are far better off remaining single throughout their lives. Our society frowns upon those who are not in relationships and although these people may be quite happy to remain single, they can feel pressurized into marrying either before they are ready to, or indeed, despite needing and wanting a solitary existence.

Loneliness and lack of self-esteem are not cured by marriage. It is much better to stay single than to get married in order to 'cleanse' yourself of feelings of inadequacy. While we are feeling bad about ourselves we are less likely to choose partners whom we truly deserve. Women are especially prone to looking at themselves in a poor light, particularly when young and this is one of the dangers of emotional immaturity.

If you do not value yourself highly enough, you are less likely to pick a partner who treats you well and you will continue to punish yourself by marrying someone who you know will make life stressful, complicated and difficult. How can these unions work in the long term? Every one of us deserves respect and honesty.

EMOTIONAL ILLNESSES

Anorexia and Bulimia

Much has been written and discussed in regard to these conditions but it is surprising how many people can suffer from emotional illnesses without ever realizing it or seeking help for their condition. The most important thing to consider is that many of those who experience these conditions are too 'ashamed' to admit to them and therefore do not seek help until someone else remarks upon it.

Depriving yourself of food to the point where you feel ill and weak, or vomiting what you eat, are emotionally and physically damaging methods of trying to bring about weight loss. It is generally felt that people suffering from these conditions have emotional problems and have feelings of low self-worth. Purging yourself of food can bring about a feeling of achievement, as though by vomiting one was cleansing away all the pain and self-loathing and promoting a feeling of value and self-control. In fact, the opposite is true. If you have ever tried to starve yourself as a form of 'punishment', or have binged on food then immediately thrown up afterwards, then you must seek help. The first person to see is your GP, who can advise you where to go for treatment. Do not expect your condition to disappear overnight, but anorexia and bulimia can be successfully treated and many people have experienced great relief to discover that this condition is not rare and there are sufferers everywhere.

Young women, especially those in early marriage, do not always adjust well to their new found 'status'. Fears of inadequacy can lead to a whole minefield of emotional problems, especially when the sense of responsibility begins to dawn. But remember, you are not alone and you do not have to suffer in silence or hide your condition as though it were something to be ashamed of. Admitting you have a problem is the best beginning towards successful recovery.

Jealousy

We all experience feelings of jealousy at different times in our lives. This feeling can range from mild envy to obsessive paranoia. It is one of the most destructive emotions we may ever feel and in its extreme form may lead to mental breakdown.

If you or your partner are experiencing feelings of jealousy which are having an adverse effect on your lives, here are some points to consider.

- Throughout our lives we will always come across those we believe to be lesser or greater than ourselves.

  It is easy to become resentful of people whom we perceive to have been bestowed with better gifts than us. But we cannot change the beauty, style, intelligence or kindness of other people. In fact we are powerless to change anything about those around us. Jealousy is a very wasteful feeling. It leads to nothing.

- Jealousy is insecurity.

  If you are not fully aware of your own attributes, and are prone to low self-esteem, almost everyone around will appear to be 'better' than you, in some way. There is no point in trying to have something that someone else has got. If you are not fully acquainted with the object of your jealousy you may be surprised to discover that they are just as insecure as you are.

- Self-confidence is the antidote to jealousy.

  If you can train yourself to accept what you are and learn to love yourself, jealousy becomes a less potent force. We have all been made differently and each one of us has something entirely unique and beautiful about us. Do not worry unnecessarily about what you think other people have. Instead look at your own good points, both in your character and your appearance, emphasize them and be proud of them.

- No-one can live with a jealous partner.

  Their constant accusations and attempts to belittle you will make it impossible for you to be happy with them. Never interpret jealousy as love. If someone demands to be with you all the time and to know what you have been doing every second you are not together, then that person needs professional help. A secure person will trust you to live your life as you choose and will not resent you having friends and acquaintances outside the relationship. A truly jealous partner can become so enmeshed in their own fantasies that they will do everything in their power to minimize your contact with people other than themselves.

- It plays no part in a happy marriage.

If you have a jealous partner and you believe their jealousy to be unfounded, then insist that they get help for it before you get married. Do not be misled into thinking that convincing them that you are faithful and that you love them will satisfy them. It won't. A jealous person will find excuses to accuse you of anything because the root of their jealousy is in their own mind. There really is nothing you can do to allay their fears because their fears are self-created. Think very carefully before committing yourself to a jealous partner. They can be hell to live with.

LOVING YOURSELF

Until you learn to love and accept yourself, you cannot love and accept someone else. The increased reporting of domestic violence is an indication of how women are now learning not to accept the abuse which they once almost took for granted.

However, women can be as capable as men of meting out abuse although not always in the same way. Most women, when consumed with anger and low self-worth, tend to direct their pain inwards upon themselves, but increasingly they are learning how to express negative emotions. These emotions, although not bad in themselves, can be badly misdirected, sometimes towards children.

Relationships in which the couple either physically and/or verbally abuse each other are those where the relationship has not altered to coincide with the changes in the couple as individuals. These people have an inability to communicate properly and in an attempt to have themselves heard and understood, lash out in aggression. How better to develop good communication between you, right at the very beginning.

If you feel that low self-esteem is having a damaging effect on your life or that of your family, then seek professional help. There are counselling services available on the NHS and they will help in the treatment of a range of emotional disorders.

It is difficult to be completely open and honest and it is important to keep some of our thoughts to ourselves. However, being able to express yourself and be understood is vital, as is development of the skill to truly listen to what your partner is saying – and where possible to read between the lines.

Avoid long periods of introspection. It is in giving that we receive and being caught up in your own thoughts all the time can be damaging to yourself and your relationship. Happy self-awareness is important, but always searching inwards will make you appear cold and unfriendly. Bear in mind the effect it can have on other people, particularly when you are always reaching a negative conclusion.

PHYSICAL ILLNESS

In later years, when our bodies start to fail us, we will have to rely on our partner's help and support. It is a fallacy to assume that we will always be healthy, either physically, emotionally or mentally.

Young couples about to marry should talk openly and honestly about their later years together. Most of us have older, infirm relatives and at least know of someone who has suffered either mental or physical breakdown. We tend to assume that these problems always affect other people. But illness and infirmity can happen at any time.

The true test of love and care comes about when one partner is ill. Ask yourself how much you would be prepared to sacrifice in order to help take care of a partner who was incapable, either for a short or long period, of taking care of themselves. If you yourself became ill, could you rely on your partner to take over the responsibility of the home and perhaps care for you as well?

It is not a pleasant thought, but one which should be debated nevertheless. Many happy couples have come through one or both partners suffering dreadful illnesses and it has made their marriage stronger and better. Do you think that is what would happen to yours? Think about it and discuss it together. Remember, ill health affects us all at some time in our lives and we will need support from loved ones. When you marry, you commit yourselves to provide each other with that support.

Look After Yourself

Although ill health affects us all in varying degrees and at different times, when we marry we have a responsibility towards ourselves and our partner to stay as healthy as we possibly can.

No-one can predict when illness is going to occur but bear in mind the maintenance of good health and the role it plays in the long-term success of your marriage.

Remember that when you get ill, your partner is as affected by it as you are. Sometimes it feels better to be ill yourself than to watch someone you love suffer. Life will throw at us what it will, but there are certain points to consider if you want to do all you can to ensure that you have a long life together.

Smoking

Generally speaking our social habits do change after we marry and to a certain extent they should. If you were accustomed to smoking forty cigarettes a day when single, do you think it wise to continue doing that after you get married?

If you and your partner both smoke then bear in mind that your health is dangerously at risk and although you may not feel the ill effects of it in your youth, you certainly will in later life. Everybody knows these facts now, but there is no better put down to romance than a lover with a hacking cough.

However, do not attempt drastically to alter a habit too early in your marriage. The stress of stopping can make people unbearable to live with. If you both smoke, try stopping together, but choose the time to do it carefully. Add it to your future diary and plan for it.

Alcohol

For the majority of people social drinking is a pleasurable activity, enhancing leisure time and relieving certain amounts of stress. Having a romantic meal in a favourite restaurant with a good bottle of wine is a great way of enjoying each other's company and can be a useful aid to lowering sexual inhibition.

However, when we are young and single we tend to enjoy

pubs and clubs and most young people spend quite a lot of time socially drinking. This is fine when pocket and energy reserves can afford it but generally speaking after marriage the way in which we choose to drink does and should change.

Alcohol is a mood-altering substance. Taken in large amounts it has an overall detrimental effect on our bodies and minds. It is important to consider the role that it plays in your life. Getting drunk every weekend may be alright when you are living alone or with flatmates but it does not make for good, loving, one-to-one relationships.

Take a long hard look at how much you drink, where, when, the frequency and effect. This demands quite rigorous honesty. If you are satisfied that alcohol is not and never has been a problem for you, then fine.

However, if it is the first thing you turn to at times of stress and difficulty, then try looking for an alternative. If you are about to get married, then you must consider your health and general well-being, not just for your own sake but for that of your partner. Alcohol abuse can become a problem for some people and many marital traumas have resulted simply because one or both partners had too much to drink.

Traditionally men have been the main perpetrators of alcohol-induced conflict, but as more and more women take control of their own finances and are experiencing the kind of work pressures that were previously only experienced by men, so the incidence of alcohol abuse in women has risen.

There are organizations that can help if you feel that alcohol is or is likely to become a problem for you. But firstly it is important to look carefully at your own levels of consumption. Violence, infidelity and accidents can all result because of overindulgence and these do not make for a happy marriage.

Food

It is common for newly married people to alter their body weight. This is usually because we want to increase our sensuous activities and eating is one of them. Cooking for each other can be great fun, as can eating out and trying new things. Eating together can be marvellous way of improving our joint activities and couples should endeavour, when possible, to eat at a table facing each other, without television or music and use meal times to discuss each other's day and listen to each other's worries, hopes and anxieties.

But food is a strangely emotive subject and can become a problem for some people. When we are first together we are inclined to overspend on food and women especially tend to cook too much for their new husband as a way of gaining his approval. Yet again, things which we enjoy in our youth, taken throughout our lives can have a damaging effect on our health.

Everything is fine in moderation. But it is better for you both to develop healthy eating habits at the beginning of your marriage than to be forced to introduce them later on when radical change will be more difficult to implement.

Most of us are pretty well educated as to what constitutes a healthy diet and what does not. We all overeat occasionally but a high-fat, high-salt diet has been proven to be a major contributor towards heart disease.

It is hard to imagine having serious heart trouble or any major illness, while still in your twenties, but the earlier we start prevention, the better. Apart from keeping our heart tissue lean, healthy eating keeps our bodies healthy and supple and the better we feel about our body image the more we can enjoy our sexual activity.

If you were raised on steak pies and suet puddings, it does not mean that you have to eat them throughout your life. If your job is sedentary you must match your eating habits to it. Also, most people find that as they get older, calories are harder to burn off.

We are all different in frame, shape and size and our family history can mean we are more likely to develop certain conditions. But healthy eating makes people feel better generally, provides more energy and can even improve powers of concentration and memory.

You do not have to eat the same types of food: my own husband is an ardent carnivore and I am a strict vegetarian. We have learned to compromise with this and just because we have differing dietary needs does not make meal times less pleasant.

Work

How and when we choose to work has an enormous influence on our feelings of self-worth and therefore on all our relationships.

Careers advice at school is sometimes woefully inadequate and many people have spent years of their lives doing a job of work which left them feeling unsatisfied, resentful and inevitably bitter.

For most people, working is essential for economic survival and unless wealth is inherited or won, working is the only way we can ensure an acceptable standard of living.

However, with the rapid changes occurring in our society and the availability of retraining and adult education, more people are finding that either through choice or necessity they are having to rethink work and careers, often at times in their lives when they least expect to.

In the relationship between work and good health, it is important to try to keep stress levels at a minimum. Some jobs are more stressful than others, but when choosing a career, bear in mind that there is stress in every job and take at look at how much you feel you are capable of coping with. Some people thrive in a high-pressure environment and others are incapable of taking more than a modicum of responsibility.

Leaving aside economic factors, you should consider your own needs. If you believe you have the personality to cope with a job that involves working unsociable hours, travelling, or dealing with the public, then so be it. Some people enjoy seeing different faces through the course of their day and others like the security of forming working relationships which may last for years. We are all different and have varying needs and skills.

It can sometimes take us a few years to come to terms with the fact that the job we are doing is putting too much stress on us as it conflicts with our personality needs. Do not let material gain be your only concern. If overwork is putting too much strain on yourself and/or your partner, rethink your position. Do not take on huge financial responsibilities which tie you to one chosen career for many years. Your needs are likely to change and although it is important to plan for the future – especially if you have or are intending to have children – you should not let worries about tomorrow prevent you from appreciating today. Invest and save by all means, but be aware of your limitations. Our lives are shorter than we think.

SUMMARY

- The more feelings of self-worth we experienced as single people, the better the chances of our marriage succeeding.

- Loneliness and lack of self-esteem are not cured by marriage; in fact, marriage may make these feelings worse.
- If you do not value yourself highly enough, you are less likely to pick a partner who treats you well. Cycles of abuse run in families.
- Emotional illnesses such as anorexia, bulimia, profound jealousy or compulsive neurosis are best treated *before* marriage is entered into. People suffering from these and other similar conditions may need quite long periods of care and rehabilitation.
- Physical and/or mental illness can occur at any time and can afflict anyone, even young people.
- Ask yourself if you would be prepared to look after a sick partner. If so, for how long?
- Do you think your partner would take care of you, if the situation arose? Talk about it.
- You have a responsibility to yourself and also to your loved ones to look after your own health. Change your habits if they are adversely affecting your health or are likely to do so in the future.
- Think carefully before embarking on a job or a career which may cause you and your family high levels of stress. Remember, your well-being directly affects those around you, especially your partner, and money does not always compensate for the destabilization of family life.

EIGHT

Family and Friends

When first married most couples feel the need to be together almost exclusively, especially if they have never lived together before. It can seem as though the outside world does not exist and that all that matters is the relationship.

We find each other interesting and exciting and it is fun discovering new things together. We know we have come through a rite of passage and we want to be left to explore our new circumstances. Other people can seem like an intrusion into the holy sanctum of our love. But the world does not go away once we become part of a couple. Our society may have pushed us together in the first place and it will continue to intervene in most aspects of our lives.

When the initial romance and euphoria have somewhat waned, we start to need increased interaction with outside friends and relatives. It is important to maintain contact with other people and it can enrich and improve your relationship. Single friends may not always understand the need of the new couple to exclude them from their lives and if friendships are to be maintained it helps to be aware that friends can sometimes feel rejected.

IN-LAWS

As discussed in Chapter 3, it is becoming increasingly difficult to stay in the town or county of our birth, if we want to take full advantage of career opportunities.

Many young couples find themselves having to move away from their families and start their married lives in strange towns. Therefore the influence of in-laws upon modern marriage has radically altered and sometimes we may have minimal contact with our parents or those of our spouse. This can have both positive and negative consequences depending on the relationship we have with our individual families.

However certain criteria still apply if you do not want family influences to have a detrimental effect on your relationships.

It is a fact that we tend to be attracted to people with similar family backgrounds to ourselves. People from families in which all the children are the same sex, for example, are inclined to marry those also from single-sex families. We bring into our own marriage the traditions and experiences of our parents' relationship. But it must be borne in mind that by virtue of the age difference, their views, attitudes and even morality are bound to be somewhat different from our own.

You cannot expect your own relationship to mirror that of anyone else. What enables some couples to live happily together for many years may be detrimental to the survival of another. What you are aiming for is a set up which suits you both and may not always have the approval of one or both sets of parents.

Equally, you should not expect to care for each other's family the way you care for your own. You do not have to become close to your in-laws just because they are your partner's parents. Respect them and endeavour to make friends with them, but do not expect to have the same sense of loyalty towards them as you have to your own family.

There may always be an element of division between one set of parents and another, but this division does not have to be dragged into your own relationship. Do not be too harsh in your criticism of your partner's family – remember that although they may be appear to be different from yours, that does not make them always wrong. Respect your partner's need to maintain whatever level of contact with them that he/she requires. You may not always fully understand this but neither do you have to. Just accept them for what they are and hopefully you can learn to like and trust them as much as you do your own family.

However, if you feel that your in-laws are having a detrimental effect on your marriage, consider your evidence carefully before attacking them. Talk to your partner about your misgivings with patience and honesty and try to explain your point of view.

Loyalty

Ultimately your loyalty should be to your partner above all else, but problems can arise when parents become over-involved in the lives of their adult children. Many women feel in conflict with their mothers-in-law as both have difficulty in adjusting to the fact that they love the same man and may have differing opinions as to how he should be treated. The relationship between mothers and sons is complex and deep, as it is with fathers and daughters and parents may intrude in the belief that what they are doing is for the benefit of their own offspring.

There are times when some things are better left unsaid. When in-laws become a problem you will know, but try to handle this situation delicately. Families can induce all sorts of conflicting emotions and predicaments. Bear in mind that whatever you may feel, they are your partner's family and although his/her loyalty should always be with you first, they may also have a strong sense of duty to their own blood relatives.

Take turns to visit each other's family and plan your visits carefully. When you have children of your own, you will need the occasional presence of other family members and they will usually expect it. In-laws can become marvellous allies and provide an additional support system when it is needed. In times of illness and bereavement whole families may join together in support of one another and although you may feel that you do not need them now, that may not always be the case.

Jealousy

Do not attempt to destroy the family bonds of your partner and try not to feel jealous if you think their ties to each other are too strong. It takes time for people to understand each other and to find their own position within the overall framework of the family. As a new member of the family, it is easy to feel left out at their gatherings. Tell your partner if you are experiencing these feelings and ask for support: your partner can guide you through the early 'getting to know each other' phase.

Parental Disapproval

If your parents strongly disapprove of your choice of partner, it is up to them to come to terms with your decision. Most parents want the best for their children but do not always express this properly. You do not have control over their feelings and attitudes.

It will make your marriage easier if you have the blessing of your parents, but if you do not, although it may cause you a great deal of pain, do not think of rejecting your partner or attempting to change him or her just to get the approval of your family. You have chosen to be together and eventually, given time and patience your parents may come to respect your choice. But if they do not, it is out of your control and you will just have to accept their opinion and get on with your relationship.

CONTINUING BAD CYCLES

For Women

When we choose with whom and when to fall in love and marry, we bring with us all the experiences of our own upbringing. Bad cycles of abuse and emotional reticence tend to be passed down from generation to generation, so although you may feel you are in control of your own desires, you may inadvertently be seeking to continue the pattern that you have been raised with, even though this pattern may be very bad indeed. Young girls who are accustomed to an absentee or abusive father frequently marry men who will also abuse them and their children. It is very important to be aware of bad cycles in your own family before choosing to marry.

Our image of ourselves can be affected by the love and approval (or lack of it) that we experienced as children. Some women who had horrific childhoods with fathers who meted out punishment and disapproval continue the pattern by falling for men who they know will treat them just like Daddy used to. This happens when a woman interprets love through her own experiences and does not believe that she deserves to be treated better. She may think that she is 'not good enough' to have wholehearted love, approval and kindness from any man and will therefore seek the kind of relationship where she knows she will get what she thinks is love – and so the pattern continues.

There is no reason why any woman (or man) should put up with abuse in a relationship. Unfortunately there are many people who do not know of anything different and come to expect it in their lives. If you are about to marry someone who has shown any signs that he may become an abuser, then put a halt on the relationship and have a long hard look at your emotional history and your self-image.

You may think you are 'in love' with this man and believe that his temper is a sign of his strength. You may even feel secure in a relationship like this because you are experiencing what you know best and are comfortable with it. But there are several important factors to be taken into account: you will not be able to change him; he needs professional help; you are not his 'rescuer' and you do not deserve to be mistreated.

Women who choose to marry men like this eventually realize that living with them is impossible. You may not always spot an abusive partner and he may not turn to abuse until after you are married, but if you have any suspicions that he is likely ever to harm you or your children wilfully then do not marry him. This is even more important if you had an abusive father: you may just be part of a bad cycle which is difficult but not impossible to break. Do not allow your own children to be brought up with the fear and disapproval that marked your life. Learn to appreciate goodness in people and do not think that every kind man you meet is a wimp or is weak.

A truly strong and capable man will never harm you and you do not have to accept bad behaviour in someone just because you are 'in love' and feel compelled to stay with him. Ask yourself *honestly* if you feel that you deserve to be treated better by your partner. If the answer is yes, then take positive steps to do something about it, preferably before you are married and have children to consider as well as yourself. Your Dad is still your Dad and your partner is still your partner, but outside of their relationship with you they are individuals with their own thought processes which may not always be healthy and balanced, whether you love them or not.

For Men

The relationship between mothers and sons is complex and varied but not always healthy. Whether we like it or not we are influenced by our upbringing and men are less likely to try and decipher bad emotional patterns than women and are therefore more likely to perpetuate them. As a man about to marry, you must assess your relationship with your own mother, especially if you experienced abuse, disapproval or emotional reticence. It will have an affect on how you treat your wife, whether you are aware of it or not.

If you are perfectly happy with your family set up, then you have no need to be concerned, but if you harbour resentments against your mother or indeed have too much dependence on her, then you are going to carry those bad cycles into your marriage. Bear in mind that your feelings for your wife are influenced by your feelings for your mother; the two are not separate but actually quite closely linked.

Do not expect your wife to carry on the relationship you have with your mother, with sex thrown in. You must learn to treat them differently and not confuse your feelings for both, as this can have a disastrous effect on your marriage.

If you are aware that there have been problems in your family, then seek to alter the pattern in your new relationship. Wives are not mothers. They are not there to look after you and care for you no matter how you behave or what you do. Also, a young woman in love may not feel emotionally strong enough to stand up to you, but that will change in time. Do not expect her to accept bad behaviour from you throughout your married life, as she has a lot of changes to go through in terms of her own growth and maturity.

If your mother abused you in any way, you may feel compelled to alter the balance in your marriage and your wife may suffer because you have latent feelings of anger for your mother. Seek to come to terms with anger or dependence or any kind of bad cycle in your relationship patterns. Being aware of them is the first step. They do not have to be perpetuated, but if they are they may ultimately cost you the chance to have a fulfilling and equal partnership with your wife and a sensible attitude to women in general.

FRIENDS

To a certain extent the same sense of dividing loyalties that are experienced with families can also be felt with friends.

It is important to maintain friendships throughout your marriage. Although your choice of friends may change as you do, it is wrong to expect your partner alone to provide you with all the mental stimulation that you need.

The best friendships are those that are based on respect and trust. You may find that a friend of your own sex can provide a different type of support than that which you get from your partner. Having other people to interact with can help to make your relationship more interesting, especially after the first few years together.

However, a good friend should always be careful regarding their demands on their married friends. If a lot of your friends are single or divorced they may resent you joining what appears to be a married persons' club and they can feel left out of your activities. As with parents, your loyalties should lie with your partner and friends should not be encouraged to visit when they like, or call around without ringing to check that you are free to spend time with them.

If certain friends are becoming demanding of your time and not respecting your need to be alone together then you must talk to them about it. Good friendships are always punctuated by periods of separation and should never become clinging and dependent. If you feel that either your own or your partner's friends are having a detrimental effect on your marriage, curtail the friendship. A true friend will understand your needs and will always be there for you when you need them.

Do not be overly concerned about having to 'let go' of a friendship which is damaging you in any way. Just because you have known someone for a long time or you have mutual shared experiences, do not let a sense of loyalty prevent you from standing up for yourself if you genuinely feel that the friendship has become an area of resentment or friction in your life.

Bad Friendships

Good friends are few but it is easy to let bad friendships dictate your decisions out of a fear of letting go of them or because you do not want to incur the anger of a so-called friend. Friends should be supportive, loving people, but friendships, like any other relationship can cause pain, frustration and anger. Be brave in your dealings with your friends, especially when you are first married. If a friend loves you, they will accept you and support your decisions. They will not deride you or criticize you to others. Friendships, like love affairs, can be chosen and can also be let go of when they become a source of rancour, jealousy or pain.

Mixed Doubles

It is also possible to have great friends of both sexes. If your partner is jealous because of a particular friendship you may have, then include them in the friendship, but try to help them to understand that they must learn to trust you. You must not abandon all your single friends after you get married because you are frightened that they will make a pass at your partner.

If they do, they were a worthless friend anyway and if your partner responds you are better off without them.

SUMMARY

- The world does not go away when you become part of a couple, even though it may seem so in the first few months you are together.
- It is important to maintain contact with other people – and doing so can enrich and improve your relationship with your partner.
- We tend to attract people from similar family backgrounds; this similarity can help us to understand each other's needs.
- You cannot expect your relationship to mirror that of anyone else, either that of your own parents or of friends.
- Do not expect to care about your in-laws as much as your partner does. Try to befriend them as much as possible and in time you may learn to love them.
- Your loyalty must always be to your partner, especially in the early years of your relationship.
- If you do not get on with your partner's family, be judicious in your criticism of them. They are, after all, the parents of the person you love.
- Do not attempt to destroy your partner's family bonds and try not to feel jealous if you think their ties to each other are too strong.
- If either or both sets of in-laws strongly disapprove of your choice, it is up to them to come to terms with your decision.

- Patterns of abuse tend to be passed down through the generations. Being aware of this is the first step towards preventing it from continuing.
- The best friendships are those that are based on mutual respect and trust. Good friendships are punctuated by periods of separation.
- Do not be frightened of 'letting go' of any relationship, either with a family member or a friend, that is damaging you in any way. Do not let a sense of loyalty prevent you from standing up for yourself and what you believe in.

NINE

Guidelines for Communication

Learning to communicate properly is an essential part of learning to live together. Being able to talk honestly and openly about your fears, dreams, shortcomings and hopes will help to build trust between you both. It does not mean that you must tell each other absolutely everything on the first date, but gradually get accustomed to making relevant points when a particular subject important to you crops up.

SECRETS

There is nothing wrong with keeping a sense of mystery or deciding that there are certain things which you do not want him/her to know. But if a secret or past indiscretion is going to bother you, then you would be wise to let the other person know about it. Common 'secrets' which have a habit of coming out later are:

- An adopted baby.
- An abortion.
- A history of sexually transmitted disease.
- A criminal record.
- Scholastic failure.
- Previous marriage.
- Mental breakdown.
- Rape/sexual assault.

- Perceived 'bad' family history.
- Some form of homosexual experience.

These are just a few of the examples of supposed secrets which couples considering marriage do not want their new partner to know about. These listed are perhaps amongst the most familiar reasons for keeping quiet, but the irony is that all of the above are quite common and may eventually come out into the open anyway, perhaps by the indiscretion of someone outside the relationship.

If you feel that a 'secret' will become a burden to keep, then think seriously about talking it over with *someone* although not necessarily your partner. It is your history and you are perfectly entitled to keep it to yourself. The only time that you should definitely consider telling a new partner about some aspect of your past, is if you feel it may at some stage have an effect upon the new relationship. But always bear in mind, that if you have experienced any of the above you are one of thousands of other people who have gone through the same thing.

GETTING TO KNOW EACH OTHER

Here are some tips about how and where to get your point across. Try to employ these *before* you get married. If you get accustomed to being honest right at the beginning it will be easy to perpetuate it. Start out lying and you may find yourself lying forever. To prevent bad patterns being laid down for the future, therefore, consider these points.

Where and When to Complain
Everyone will find at some stage in their relationship that they

have something which they feel justified in complaining about. But no matter what the subject and despite how important it may be to you, you must think carefully about where and when you voice your complaints. There is no point, for instance in calling your partner at work to complain about some aspect of their behaviour. If your partner is busy, they will only be annoyed to have been interrupted and they will not be able to speak openly with you anyway. Try and hold your tongue until you are both at home. If you want not only to have your point listened to but to be understood and accepted, then it is best to time your words, until the recipient has eaten, is relaxed and you have privacy to talk.

Get Out of Your Normal Environment

If you really want the undivided attention of someone else, try and remove them from the home environment for a couple of hours. A quiet café or restaurant is a good place to talk to each other, as long as you don't intend having a slanging match. You will be listened to if your partner has little or no other stimulation. They have to be attentive if you are the only person speaking and they can't switch on the television, pick up a paper or go to bed. Restaurants are good places for patching up all sorts of small problems, because you will probably be seated opposite each other and have to behave with a modicum of self-restraint.

Let's Talk About Sex

If you are having sexual problems, the bedroom is NOT the place to discuss them, particularly if you want to complain. The best place for a discussion about sex is outside. Go for a long walk and talk as you walk. Talking about sex can be very difficult so if you are going to have an in-depth discussion about your most intimate lives, plan the conversation and raise the subject when it will be unexpected but listened to without other stimuli. Parks are excellent places to talk about such matters as the sense of freedom and movement can make expression easier than when one is indoors. Try it, it is surprisingly effective.

Later On
The point of choosing where and how to complain is to remove the home base as the main source. You do not want your partner to associate your home with conflict and upset. If you can, try and raise difficult subjects when you are out of the home but still have time and privacy to talk. By the time you get home, particularly if you have walked, it will be easier to imagine that you have left your problems elsewhere and are returning to a place of peace and solace.

  If you do not have the financial wherewithal to go out every time you need to talk, then ask a neighbour to babysit so that you are free to walk around the block. The important thing is to change your surroundings when you can. Do not make rows and recriminations an element of your home life, if you can possibly avoid it.

How to Approach a Difficult Subject
Once you have chosen the time and the place in which to raise your disagreement, you must think carefully as to how you will approach it. Shouting, screaming and accusing are not effective tools to employ and will, in fact, get you nowhere. If you want really to be effective in your complaints, choose your words carefully. We cannot always plan when we are going to be angry, but if something has been bothering you for some time and you feel the need to get it into the open, then planning is of the essence. This may seem like strange advice, but when you say something is as important as how you say it.

After you have decided when and where to raise the subject, then think very carefully about your partner's point of view, before you actually speak to them. If, for example, you are a woman who is concerned about a partner who may be drinking too much, instead of launching into an attack on his behaviour try and think of reasons why he needs to do this, if it has been controlled in the past.

There are two sides to everything and if you are aware that what you are going to say will cause pain and recrimination, then it would be wise to seek information from other sources before attacking your partner first and foremost.

Be careful who you are angry with. If your boss has been giving you a hard time or you have had an argument with a friend, do not be tempted to take out your anger and frustration on your partner. It is sometimes easier to hurt those we love most, but it is a coward's way out. If you are unhappy at work, sort it out at work, do not bring it home and make your partner's life a misery by niggling at them all evening.

Whatever the subject, find out as much as you can, plan your time and words and then gently ease the subject into the conversation. A good way to start is to ask if anything is wrong. Do not pry, you want information but you will not get it by interrogation. Tell your partner that you have noticed something about their behaviour which is worrying you and that you are concerned about it. Give them space and time to think about what you have said. Let them slowly realize that you are unhappy, instead of shoving it in their face.

Criticism

Bear in mind that most people are highly sensitive to criticism. No-one likes to be reminded of their shortcomings and certainly not by the one person whom they expect to support them at all times. Think carefully about the subject matter of your disagreement. Remember that you may not be aware of all the facts. It can take years before people feel fully free to divulge some things from their past, but they bring these things into their relationship with you whether you like it or not.

Some people are very paranoid about being discovered as being less than perfect and having all the right answers. But none of us are perfect. There are also some things which are really better left unsaid.

Learning to Express Yourself Properly

People who have difficulty with communicating verbally may turn to other forms of communication, which can lead to abuse and even violence. Not all of us are gifted with a large vocabulary or have the emotional maturity to make a complaint adequately without causing undue harm. But it is important for you to understand the power of careful and controlled self-expression. When two people have a row they tend to exaggerate their thoughts in the heat of the moment and may frequently say the most hurtful things which they really don't mean.

If you have genuine difficulty explaining how you feel and are nervous about expressing your opinions in the wrong way, the most useful tool to employ is a pen. When you feel really angry and frustrated, write down your feelings. Look at them in black and white and it will give you a better idea of what you are experiencing. If you feel incapable of saying these things to your partner, write to them. We cannot always say what we are thinking but writing down our feelings and fears goes a long way towards helping us to come to terms with them. Show your partner what you have written. Ask them to take a few days to think about it and await their reaction.

Dutch Courage

Never use alcohol or drugs to give you the courage to complain to someone, either your partner or anyone else. You will not be able to judge your own reactions, nor theirs and false sentimentality and histrionics are more likely to ensue than balanced, thoughtful and healthy debate.

Courage is an important factor in learning to express yourself properly, but so is a degree of introspection. Think very carefully about what you want to say. We are surrounded with images of people expressing their opinions in a negative and destructive manner. You are perfectly entitled to voice fears but be wary of exaggerating your partner's inadequacies.

Once you have said something damaging and hurtful you cannot take it back, it is already too late. Frustration can lead to all sorts of menacing action, including physical violence, but violence does not have to be physical to be expressed. Words can sometimes hurt even more, so be careful. Remember that you intend to continue living with another individual and although it is vital that you learn how to express yourself at the right time, use the least damaging language you can muster.

Screaming matches really do lead to nothing. Everyone has rows, they are inevitable, but how much better it is if you can teach yourself to get your point across without causing unnecessary pain or inflicting wilful damage that you may not be able to repair.

Gathering Information

If you feel that your relationship is suffering because of something which is outside your control then seek help from the relevant agencies before trying to tackle serious problems yourself. Depression, stress, alcohol, drug abuse, violence, debt and emotional disorders are examples of problems for which there are networks of support and advice services available. If you think your partner may be suffering from any of these disorders which go way beyond your ability to cope, then before confronting him/her talk to a professional. Your GP is always the first port of call and he/she can guide you in the right direction.

Most couples suffer more from the bad effects of outside influences than they do from problems between each other and it is important for you to differentiate between relationship problems and life problems. Even couples who dearly love and care for each other can find the stresses and strains of modern life permeating into their relationship and causing problems between them which have a detrimental effect on the marriage.

It is impossible to co-exist if one of you is suffering from any kind of serious disorder and care should be taken in approaching an ill or disturbed person. We none of us are perfect, but there are certain things over which the partner of an individual is completely powerless.

Do not blame yourself or necessarily the other person every time something goes wrong between you. Gathering information is a vital means by which you can help and understand each other. Before you decide to attack a partner who you feel is neglecting you or treating you badly, make sure as far as you can that they are not suffering from problems outside your life together. They will only resent you for adding to what they see as their own worries. Remember we are each of us different and we all react to stress in completely different ways.

Information on a whole range of subjects is available in the local library, a place infrequently visited by most people. There you can find books and articles that may help you and there are also details of support groups and community projects in your area. By visiting a library and reading up on the problems you are experiencing, you are in a better position to tackle them without having to rely on family or friends to advise you.

Listening

One of the strange side effects of a loving relationship is that you can become too close. In most respects this is not a bad thing but it can cause you to push out 'bad' information when you receive it because you do not want to lose that special closeness you have. A lot of people are frightened to delve too much into their relationships in case they discover something hurtful or damaging, but if you want to have the true freedom to be yourself and to understand each other, then it is important to become adept at listening.

Sometimes we have to hear things about ourselves that we do not like or want to hear. But we tend to judge ourselves too harshly most of the time and may find that given the chance to listen to the opinion of those closest to us we can reach a better understanding of ourselves.

No two people can spend years together without arguing and disagreeing. In the first few months of married life, you do not expect to argue. People set themselves enormous challenges without realizing that you both have to find your own space in the relationship and this jostling for position will lead to arguments. When these occur, remember that it is as important to listen as it is to speak. Your partner has to feel that they can talk to you honestly without derision or rancour coming from you. Do not be too quick to criticize or jump in with counter-accusations every time you hear a complaint. Your partner may just be right. Perhaps you are lazy, untidy, self-absorbed, vain, materialistic or just plain nasty. All these things can be rectified and should be if you want to enjoy a long and happy life together.

People in the first flush of love do not like to criticize each other, but given time their misgivings will come out. It takes courage to listen to someone because you may not always like what you hear, but eventually it will do your relationship a lot of good and encourage you both to voice your opinions honestly. A balance can be struck and you will find trust building between you as a result.

You would not like to think that your partner would talk to a friend or someone at work or even a relative before they would come to you. Many people are unfaithful because they want a sympathetic listener rather than a lover. For some it is easier to turn outside of the relationship to seek solace and acceptance than it is to turn to the person to whom they are married.

If you make yourself available as a listener to your partner they are much less likely to take their fears and worries to someone else. Make them aware that you are there for them, no matter how they may be feeling and that first and foremost they have your support.

Breaking Stalemates

Sometimes in life it is necessary to put your own needs to one side in order to maintain your relationship. The degree to which you are prepared to do this is up to you. Successful co-habitation is dependent upon both being able to compromise.

But there are certain issues on which some couples simply cannot agree and in order for the stalemate to be broken and therefore for the relationship to survive, someone will just have to give in.

These can range from when and if to have children, when and where to move house, whose career takes priority and the influence of other family members. In order to resolve major areas of conflict a great deal of self-examination needs to be carried out. For example, if one of you is adamant that you do not want children and the other is desperately hoping for parenthood, you are up against a major life decision which may eventually destroy the marriage.

That is why it is vital to talk about these issues *before* you get married. People can and do change and compromise is vital to the survival of even the most happy unions.

If you have reached a stalemate and can see no way out, then seek professional counselling. You may change your mind when more information about a subject is made available to you. It is hard to imagine when you are young that in ten years time you may have altered your attitudes quite drastically. The best way to handle a stalemate is to put a time-scale on the situation and re-evaluate it at a slightly later date. Use the intervening time to examine your own attitudes. This does not mean ignore the issue and hope that it goes away because it will not, but try to find some sort of common ground between you.

After a given period, perhaps six months, resume negotiations on the subject which is causing you so much difficulty. If counselling and information-gathering has not succeeded then you have to decide if your own needs are overwhelming enough for the marriage to be able to continue. But bear in mind the possibility that selfishness and youthful arrogance may cause you to lose something which in later years you will regret.

One of the most common complaints people have about each other is stubbornness. It is difficult to find a middle ground where stubbornness becomes understanding and stalemate becomes compromise. It really depends on how important the other person is to you. It is easy to take love for granted when young, but people who divorce as a direct result of an inability to waiver from their own viewpoint frequently regret it years later. If you are in a serious stalemate, try and imagine your life ten years into the future and ask yourself if the hassle you are experiencing now is really worth it in a lifetime of incidents.

Approaching Others

When you have problems between you and you decide to seek help from elsewhere, be very careful whom you choose to approach. Your best friend or a relative may seem like the most supportive person, but they may not always advise you well. If you want sycophancy you know where to get it, but the truth is more important than partisan information. Other members of your family can step in and cause even more damage, so think carefully before telling them the details of your most intimate problems.

Sometimes the best person to look at a situation objectively is someone who is not known to all the protagonists; a minister, priest, rabbi, counsellor or doctor, for example. In other words, someone who does not have a vested interest in whether or not your marriage survives. They are trained to deal with domestic problems and are more likely to give you honest advice than someone who, for instance, may dislike your partner and advise you from that very negative standpoint.

Approaching someone outside the relationship can be terrifying. No-one wants to admit they may have a problem, but admitting to it is the first step towards rectifying it. Talking over your fears with an independent witness can help to alleviate a whole range of anxieties. It is the premise on which most self-help and support groups are run.

You may very well find that your fears are misguided and even imaginary. If you do decide to run home to Mum the minute things go wrong do not expect to get good, honest advice; in family rows blood tends to be thicker than water. And if you have gone down to the pub and told all your friends how horrible your partner is being, you are going to be mightily embarrassed if you patch up your differences when people expect you to be splitting up. Your partner may not appreciate you telling other people about the private things between you and you could end up causing more trouble than you intended.

Private Language

There is one other important point to be considered when deciding to approach other people to help you sort out your relationship difficulties. No-one can fully understand what goes on between a couple. Closely bonded people have a language and intimacy of their own which no one else is privy to and in some cases lovers can actually invent a completely new mode of speech which only the other can understand. This can be seen in the love messages published in newspapers around St Valentine's Day. Not all those people are teenagers, yet they obviously have a unique language of their own. Perhaps we develop this as a form of protection against outside influences or we are trying to create an intimate fantasy. Suffice to say, that private language exists, for whatever reason.

Therefore, it is difficult to make other people aware of your joint problems and they will advise you on the basis of your argument alone. If the person offering you advice is a member of your own family or a close friend you are unlikely to get a balanced viewpoint. Only you can decide when you need to look outside the relationship for advice.

Be Warned

You should try to avoid talking to a single friend of the opposite sex about your relationship problems. Friendships in these circumstances frequently become love affairs and if you want to stay with your partner, you would be wise to seek advice from a professional person, rather than a sexy friend. Your need to talk can be perceived as a come-on, sometimes without you even realizing it.

Professional Help

Pride can be a dangerous thing in any relationship and should never be used to prevent people seeking professional help if they need it. People are becoming more aware of the facilities available to help them, which are free to all, but there is still a stigma attached to seeking help with certain non-medical conditions, such as emotional, behavioural or psychiatric problems.

There is no point in this book advising you when and if to find professional help. Only you can tell when that time has come and it is a simple matter of control. We sometimes put too much on our own shoulders and especially in marriage we like to feel that we can always solve our problems internally, without outside help.

Control

But we do not have control over other people. The only person we can control is ourselves. If a situation at home is getting out of hand then you know it is time to look elsewhere.

Most people find the best aspect of joining a support group or talking to a counsellor is discovering that they are not alone. When we are suffering from emotional or mental disorders it is very easy to believe that we are completely alone with our suffering, whereas in fact people can react quite similarly to stressful situations in their lives and whatever the disorder, there is always someone else experiencing it.

Sometimes the most difficult part of suffering from an emotional or spiritual disorder is admitting that it even exists. Some people have been known to suffer from such problems as compulsive eating, neurotic obsessions, or agoraphobia for years without ever having discussed it with anyone or trying to seek help.

Enabling

Unfortunately some people need to have their partner dependent on them and may discourage them from seeking help for certain illnesses, because they are frightened that when the 'sick' person gets better they will no longer want to stay in the relationship.

There are varying examples of this and in its most extreme form it is very damaging indeed. In the same way that some women encourage their husbands to become dependent upon them for food and cleanliness, so some people discourage unhealthy partners to get better, because of their own fears and lack of self-worth.

For example, some women have been known to enable their husbands to drink too much so as to make them unattractive to other women and more needing of their wives. Some men have been known to become extremely angry and hurt when their previously obese wives join a slimming club and emerge as eight stone beauties. It always comes down to self-worth. If you are happy and secure with yourself you will want to be with someone who is also happy and secure. To discourage someone from getting help because of your own insecurities proves who the really sick individual is.

Myths and Legends

There are a lot of myths surrounding supposed conversations between men and women and there is a lot written about body language and the way in which we relate to each other. Most of this makes for interesting debate and occasionally a good laugh, but let's debunk some silly ideas we may have about each other.

- Men do not 'pull' women.

    A woman may talk to whom she likes whenever she likes but if she decides she is attracted to someone enough to want to spend more time, intimately or otherwise, with them, it is entirely up to her. A man who goes beyond what a women desires and forces himself sexually upon her is raping her. End of story.
- All men are bastards.

    This is a cruel and misleading statement that younger women frequently say to comfort each other after a relationship has gone wrong. If all men are bastards, why do women continue to marry them? There is good and bad in everyone. Some men are cowards and some women are users. Maintaining personal integrity in your actions towards yourself and others will bring you into less contact with nasty people. Simple.
- Men have acquaintances and women have friends.

    Again this is one of those myths which does men an enormous disservice. Men are just as capable as women of forming deep and important friendships with people of both sexes. A person's maturity and self-awareness determine how they view the other people to whom they are close and how they choose to interact with them.
- Children should be seen and not heard.

    This may seem like an outdated statement but in many homes this logic still applies. If a couple have free and honest expression between each other, their children will pick up on it and learn from it. It will enable them to grow up into secure individuals who are aware of themselves and their own opinions and are not frightened to be honest.

- Men want sex and women want love.

The real truth is that both want both. It is sometimes believed that men 'screw around' and women don't or indeed shouldn't. But the men who are supposedly 'putting it about' are doing so with women who are doing exactly the same. Men have more freedom to extol the so-called virtues of this behaviour and women tend not to talk about it in the same way. But they both do it and it is actually a means by which people can find the one person with whom they can stay with forever. It is not a good way of finding a long-term partner but it is the most common method employed by young Western people, of *both* sexes.

- If someone says 'I Love You' they mean it.

Unfortunately this phrase has become one of the biggest clichés of all time, used by all and sundry as the whim takes them. It is impossible to tell initially if someone has lied to you but if you should hear this phrase used on a first or second date, proceed with extreme caution. What the person wants to say is 'I am having a great time being with you' but 'I love you' has proved to more effective. Real love, however, is proven by actions rather than words and the simple truth is if someone loves you they will want to be with you, at any cost, as often as possible. You cannot say 'I love you' in one breath and in the next state that you are too busy to go out again for another month. People in love usually want to be together, no matter what.

Conclusion

Not every marriage breaks up and there are success stories to be found. Most of us have elderly relatives or friends who have remained married to the same person for all of their adult lives, literally 'til death do us part'. So what is happening to the relationships of today and where are we going so dreadfully wrong? Why are women, particularly, leaving their marriages so readily and in such large numbers?

The nature of marriage in Western society has changed dramatically in just one generation. This is largely the result of the change in the status and outlook of women. Most young women today have opportunities and ambitions undreamed of by their mothers and grandmothers; they have the same educational choices as their brothers, they can maintain sexual relationships without fear of pregnancy or social vilification, and they are as ambitious and forward-thinking as their male counterparts.

It's true that many young women, particularly those from disadvantaged backgrounds, still desire only to get married and have children, so seem to have been unaffected by the general change in women's consciousness; in surveys of 15-year-old girls in inner-city schools, results have shown that most still expect their lives to be completely fulfilled by their roles as wives and mothers.

Divorce, however, affects people from all walks of life, regardless of their social attitudes or degree of affluence. It is no respecter of class or social status. Even women who are less advantaged and apparently more determined to make their marriages work, are still seeking ways out, with or without children and irrespective of economic hardship.

What is it that makes marriages appear such bastions of pain and resentment that we seek to remove ourselves from them within a few short years of entering them? What happens to turn the blushing bride of 24 into the cynical divorcee of 30? Some would argue that the only reason divorce rates have risen so highly since the mid-seventies is the simple fact that legislation has made it possible and that many more people would have taken that course previously, had they had the legal support and economic wherewithal.

Obviously society no longer frowns upon divorced people and single parents do not have to suffer the social stigma that was once attached to them. But this does not alter the fact that marital breakdown causes intense suffering to adults, is damaging to children and costs the government – and therefore all of us – millions of pounds in social security payments every year.

What I have aimed to achieve in this book is to give young people a better idea of what they are likely to face in the first few years they are together, and how to respond to the changes that will inevitably occur within themselves. Staying married has never been so difficult as it is now, and unless we begin to face up to the challenges which are confronting us daily, even those couples with the best opportunities to succeed are going to fail. But it *is* possible to nurture and sustain a happy marriage, providing various issues are addressed right at the beginning of the relationship. Prevention is always better than cure and it is in self-knowledge that we learn to distinguish outer difficulties.

It is better to iron out problems while you are free of responsibility, than to try to tackle them when you have a mortgage and children to consider. The emotional investment that you make right at the beginning can pay dividends in the long term.

Some people are well advised never to marry. But most of us do marry and statistically marriage is still very popular. We are all of us entitled to the information which can help us to thrive as individuals within the framework of our relationships, while maintaining the joy and fulfilment that a happy marriage can bring. Our children deserve the best we can offer them and by looking at ourselves and our relationships before marriage and children, we are better equipped to deal with problems and set-backs as they occur and have the necessary tools to deal with them.

I would hope that this book would encourage better communication between people; if problems can be anticipated and discussed prior to them occurring, then mutual love, respect and trust can be maintained and healthy patterns for the future can be laid down. I have offered guidelines for topics which you may or may not wish to discuss – but if you are frightened to approach a certain subject with your partner at an early stage in the relationship, then you are looking for trouble. Talk, talk and more talk is required and even if it involves a few tears it may also bring laughter, honesty and freedom to be yourself.

Being aware of your own needs is another important factor. You cannot ignore them and if you try to compromise too much, inevitably a time will come when you can no longer carry this out and the result will be the demise of your relationship.

It is an increasingly common practice for young people to live together before they get married. It is assumed that in 'getting to know each other' on a daily basis they are better prepared for marriage. But it is not always the case. Some people choose to live together for economic reasons and have no intention of ever getting married. For others, living together can be seen as a statement of individuality and an unwillingness to alter a happy relationship.

This is because living together is simply not the same as being married. No matter how much you share as co-habitees and no matter how convinced you are that being married will 'feel' the same, it rarely does. While living with someone, there is a much easier 'get out' clause. You are not bound legally, unless you have children and once married, people can experience feelings of being 'trapped' which living together prevents. Even people who jointly own property and who are considered to all intents and purposes as being married, have the psychological advantage of being legally, and to a certain extent emotionally, single.

If you genuinely feel that you are not ready to get married, or that you are frightened of the changes that it might bring, or you are politically opposed to the idea, or you envisage a time when the relationship may be break down, then quite simply do not get married. To get married is to make an enormous statement, to yourself, your family and to society that you have made a decision to be bound to one other individual for the rest of your life. There is a difference between living a single life and living within marriage with a 'single mentality'. There are pros and cons to both, but it is unwise to 'try out' marriage when in your heart you know you will resent the obvious intrusion of someone else, no matter how much you love them. Our changing world has made it possible for more of us to live as we choose and choice is the key word in every decision we make.

Heartfelt commitment does not always arrive with the wedding ring; it may already be there whether you marry or not and it is the commitment to the relationship as a mode for living your life and planning your future that really matters.

No matter how open and 'modern' a couple consider

themselves to be, they may find that no amount of living together could have prepared them for the change in their relationship once the vows have been exchanged.

Some couples do not have the luxury of being 'allowed' to live together before they get married and still manage to maintain successful and loving partnerships lasting for years.

Basically, whether you live together or not, whether you are poor or rich, whether your family approve or not, does not seem to have any long-term influence on the ultimate chances of staying together and no one is immune from marital breakdown.

The key point is self-awareness. If you can remove all the factors that may inadvertently affect your decision to marry and rely instead on your own gut reactions to the situation, asking yourself honest questions about your life and how you want to live it, you then put yourself in a better position to make the right decision, primarily for yourself but also for your partner.

The size and location of the wedding, the feelings of your family and/or friends, your age or perceived status, are factors which deserve consideration but really do not have much effect on your chances of staying together. A decision to marry is an adult and individual decision – only you can make it – and your chances of survival are more dependent on honesty and communication than on any other factor.

However there are no rules, as such, for success. It depends entirely upon each individual couple how they will conduct their relationship. Some people keep a marriage together by role playing for over twenty years and then once their children have left home, their reason for staying together evaporates and they inevitably part company. Other couples get so involved in a compromise situation that one of them is constantly giving, the other is constantly taking and it is not until the 'giver' stops, that the relationship ends. Some women have a nasty habit of 'falling' for men who they know will treat them very badly indeed, and then try to turn these men into nice people, often with disastrous consequences. One can understand how an insecure person is more likely to be attracted to someone more insecure than themselves, but eventually one of them may begin to grow up and it is more than likely that the other will be left behind. 'Rescuing' someone may suit you very well now, but do you really want to be their protector and provider for the rest of your life?

However, despite fears, setbacks, family problems, poverty or division, people still want to be together. The world can seem like a terrifying place in which to live alone and we all need love and comfort to make our lives complete. Having a companion, whom you can trust, with whom you can share the grind of living is a life-enhancing experience and as our lives are so short we owe it to ourselves and our children to make our homes places of peace, security and warmth.

FINALLY

There are an increasing number of people who regret getting divorced. Most of these are men but not all. Divorce may seem like the only option when a relationship has broken down, but having spoken to many people who have experienced it, I have never heard it described as easy. It is usually painful and emotionally damaging. You do not want to find yourself, several years later, trying desperately to win back a spouse who has learnt to live without you and may be in another relationship.

Some people have been known to say 'I do not want him/her anymore but I do not want anyone else to have them'. If you cannot allow someone to be free to live their life without you, then perhaps you should think seriously about why that is.

Are you just jealous, or is there still love present there? Is splitting up the only option?

People do divorce and remarry the same person sometimes, in fact it is becoming increasingly common and divorced couples may even continue to sleep together even though they are no longer legally married. It is a shame that it can sometimes take separation to make some people realize how much they truly love and need each other. But perhaps by talking over some of the issues I have raised in this book, some people can have a better understanding of themselves *before* they get married and find some of the tools they need to sustain them, separately and collectively, in an insecure and rapidly changing world.

Further Reading

Chaplin, Jocelyn, *Love in an Age of Uncertainty*, Thorsons/Aquarian, London 1993

Cohen, David, *Being a Man*, Routledge, London 1990

De Angelis, Barbara, *Are You The One For Me?*, Thorsons, London 1993

——, *Secrets About Men Every Woman Should Know*, Thorsons, London 1992

Eysenck, H., J. Wakefield, S. Forward et al., *Men Who Hate Women and the Women Who Love Them*, Bantam Press, London 1988

Gray, John, *Men Are From Mars, Women Are From Venus*, Thorsons, London 1993

Henderson, Julie, *The Lover Within*, Thorsons/Aquarian, London 1993

Housden, Roger and Chloë Goodchild (Eds), *We Two*, Thorsons/Aquarian, London 1992

Miller, Stuart, *Men and Friendship*, Gateway Books, Bath 1983

McGinnis, Alan Loy, *The Romance Factor*, Harper San Francisco 1991

Montuori, Alfonso and Isabella Conti, *From Power to Partnership*, Harper San Francisco 1993

Papillon, Marie, *A Million and One Love Strategies*, Thorsons, London 1992

Tannen, D., *You Just Don't Understand*, Virago Press, London 1991

Tysoe, Maryon, *Love Isn't Quite Enough*, Fontana, London 1992